Songs to Sing and Picture

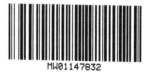

Songs to Sing and Picture

Grades PreK-2

Lillian L. Dudley
and
Harriet R. Kinghorn

1996
Teacher Ideas Press
A Division of
Libraries Unlimited, Inc.
Englewood, Colorado

TEACHER IDEAS PRESS
A Division of
Libraries Unlimited, Inc.
P.O. Box 6633
Englewood, CO 80155-6633
(800) 237-6124

Project Editor: Stephen Haenel
Layout and Design: Michael Florman
Proofreader: Suzanne Hawkins Burke

Library of Congress Cataloging-in-Publication Data

Suggested Cataloging:

Dudley, Lillian L.
Songs to sing and picture : grades preK-2 / Lillian L. Dudley, Harriet R. Kinghorn.
x, 121 p. 22x28 cm.
ISBN 1-56308-367-1
1. School songbooks. 2. Pantomime. 3. Teaching aids and devices.
I. Dudley, Lillian L. II. Kinghorn, Harriet R. III. Title.
782.542 1996
792.3
371.3078

Contents

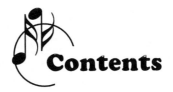

Acknowledgments

The authors wish to express their appreciation to Michael Morris for the preparation of the music. They would also like to thank Nancy L. Reed and Joy A. Ferguson for their help, suggestions, and support with this book.

Introduction

Curriculum Integration

For many years, teachers and educators have been involved in curriculum integration—combining academic subjects with other subjects—in an effort to prevent fragmentation of the overall curriculum. In response to the dynamic growth of the body of knowledge during the Age of Information, teachers in partnership with educators and parents have sought to present to learners a realistic view of the world and an integrated set of tools to prepare for lifelong learning. One aspect of this process is to relate theory and ideas to practice and experience. James B. Ingram, in his book *Curriculum Integration and Lifelong Education* (Pergamon Press, 1979), lists some of the functions of integrated learning as: coping with changes in knowledge, interrelating different areas of knowledge, providing a sense of purpose, providing a curriculum conducive to learning, promoting personality development through learning, teaching and learning through sharing, coping with interdisciplinary issues, and relating school and society.

To promote curriculum integration, the songs and activities in this book provide learners the opportunity to explore topics relevant to their interests while partnering different academic subject areas. A range of learner's interests has been considered in the preparation of the material in this book—from animals to plants, from math to science, and from riddles to songs. *Songs to Sing and Picture* allows parents and teachers to guide learners in their exploration of topics while providing sound learning experiences. The materials may be used to reinforce self-esteem, multiculturalism, home, family, and joy of learning. These concepts are the basis on which the songs and activities are built. Based on the authors' belief that the classroom is not an isolated environment, they encourage the learners to share their leaning experiences with family and friends.

Learning Objectives

There are several learning objectives emphasized in this book. One is the growth of vocabulary through rhyming, use of a dictionary, identification of words of parallel structure, and discussion of word inferences. Another is the promotion of comprehension through song lyrics, which are learned in the songs or supplied by the learner and then discussed. The book is intended to promote imagination and creativity using artistic and musical experiences integrated with classroom topics. (See topics listed on page 113.) As learners enjoy the activities, self-esteem and independent learning are encouraged and supported.

Format of the Book

Each topic is introduced by a song. After the children have learned the song, they do an activity that relates to the song. The activities include art, science, mathematics, social studies, and language arts. A book is listed on the child's song sheet for each topic. For example, *Hopscotch Around the World* by Mary D. Lankford is printed under the song "Friends Around the World." If the suggested book is not available, another book about the topic can be read. Teachers may reproduce the music sheets for one classroom only to allow learners to share their music with family and friends. Some adults or children will enjoy playing the songs on a piano, a keyboard, or on some other kind of instrument. Simple piano accompaniments for each of the songs are included. The musical sheets include simple chords for the guitar or autoharp so that the teacher or parent can accompany children. The music can be used by people of limited musical backgrounds as well as teachers of music.

Suggestions for Use

The authors offer these suggestions for enhanced use of the ideas and materials in the book. The activity and recommended book title accompanying each song can be modified for varying ages. Learners may say or sing lyrics or may write activities or contribute ideas as the teacher or parent writes. The teacher may wish to detach the activity from the reproduced song sheet and develop additional or substitute activities.

The songs can be used in partnership with movement for a school program, and the activities can be compiled into a gift for family or friends. Learners may wish to create their own songs and activities outside the classroom.

Closing Thoughts

Whether the songs in this book are accompanied by a specific activity such as drama, movement, choral reading, or writing, they may be integrated with essential classroom topics. When a new song is learned, the teacher may have learners sing it as an up-beat, closing activity. Singing a song from *Songs to Sing and Picture* is a great way to end the day!

Songs to Sing and Picture

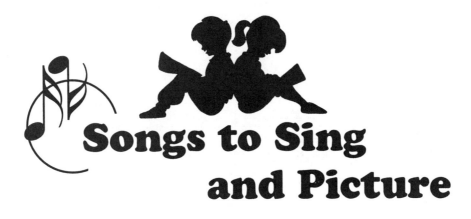

All By Myself

©1995 L. Dudley

All By Myself

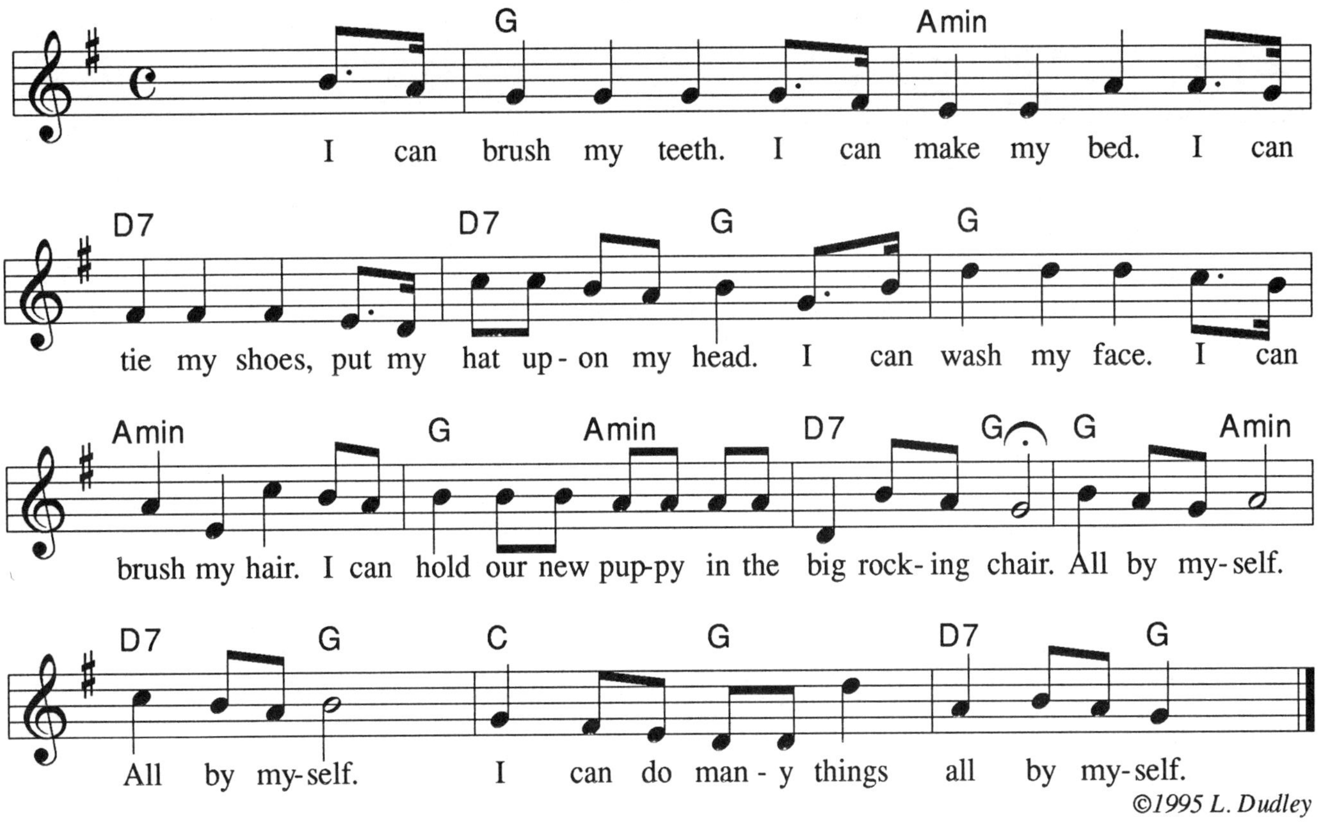
G
Amin
I can brush my teeth. I can make my bed. I can
D7
D7
G
G
tie my shoes, put my hat up-on my head. I can wash my face. I can
Amin
G
Amin
D7
G
G
Amin
brush my hair. I can hold our new pup-py in the big rock-ing chair. All by my-self.
D7
G
C
G
D7
G
All by my-self. I can do man-y things all by my-self.
©1995 L. Dudley

PANTOMIME GAME

1. Taking turns, each of you should pantomime something that you can do alone.
2. The other players should guess what you are miming.

Read *Let Me Do It!* by Janice Gibala-Broxholm or another book about things you can do alone.

Animal Riddle One

I'm a zoo an - i - mal. I can sit in a tree;
swing- ing all a- round is the life for me. I have a friend at the zoo who is
big and fat, a big long nose and feet that are flat.

Animal Riddle One

F
B♭
I'm a zoo an - i - mal I can sit in a tree;
C7
F
F
swing-ing all a-round is the life for me. I have a friend at the zoo who is
B♭
C7
C7
F
big and fat, a big long nose and feet that are flat.
©1995 L. Dudley

WHAT ANIMALS ARE WE?

Draw and color pictures to show the answers to the riddle in the song.

Read *Riddles About Animals* by Jacqueline A. Ball or another book about animals.

Animal Riddle Two

I'm a woods an - i - mal 'bout as big as a kit - ty, a
stripe down my back, I don't smell ve - ry pret - ty. There's an - oth - er an - i - mal with such
big long ears. He puts them straight up at ev' - ry thing he hears.

©1995 L. Dudley

Animal Riddle Two

F
B♭
I'm a woods an - i - mal 'bout as big as a kit - ty, a
C7
F
F
stripe down my back, I don't smell ve - ry pret - ty. There's an - oth - er an - i - mal with such
B♭
C7
C7
F
big long ears. He puts them straight up at ev' - ry thing he hears.

©1995 L. Dudley

<u>WHAT ANIMALS ARE WE?</u>

Draw and color pictures to show the answers to the riddle in the song. Write or tell one of your own animal riddles about one of the animals in the song.

Read *It Does Not Say Meow* by Beatrice Schenk de Regniers or another book about riddles.

Animal Riddle Three

I can be a pet and live in your house. I'm
ra - ther small and I look like a mouse. An - oth - er pet has
ve - ry soft fur. The sound she makes is called a purr.

©1995 L. Dudley

Animal Riddle Three

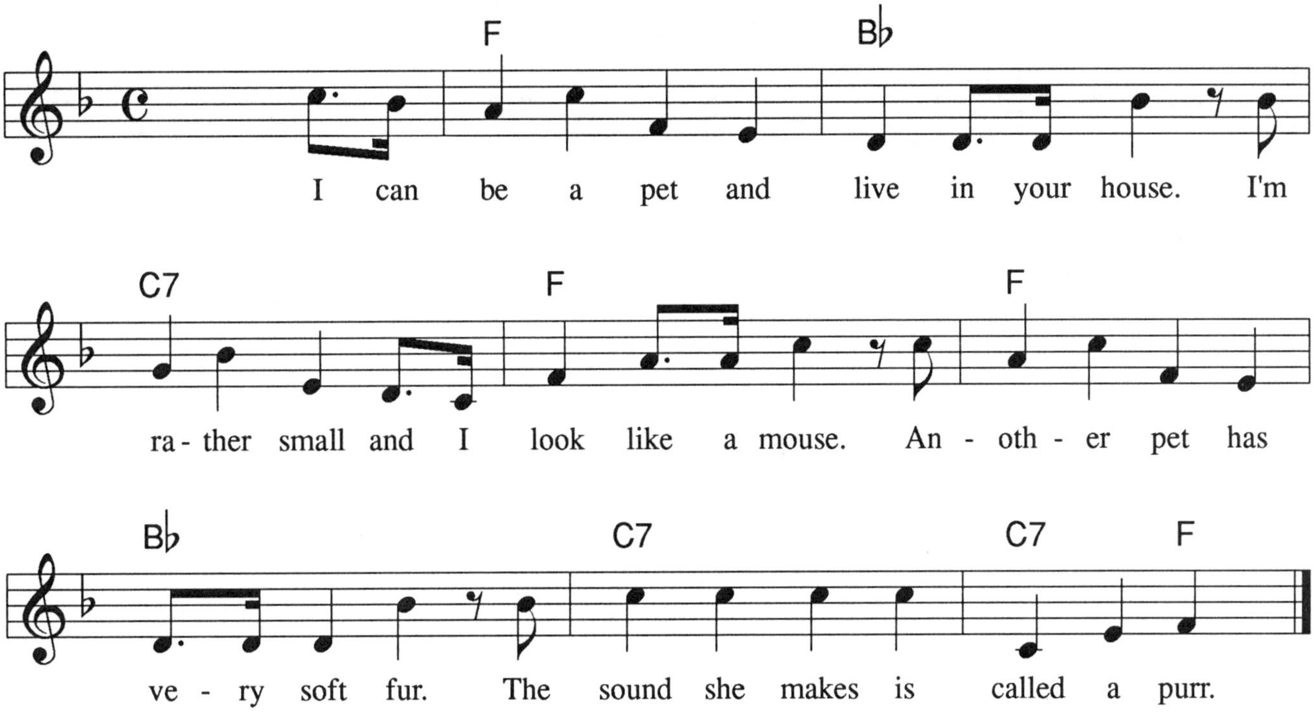
F
B♭
I can be a pet and live in your house. I'm
C7
F
F
ra- ther small and I look like a mouse. An - oth - er pet has
B♭
C7
C7
F
ve - ry soft fur. The sound she makes is called a purr.

©1995 L. Dudley

WHAT ANIMALS ARE WE?

Draw and color pictures to show the answers to the riddle in the song. Write or tell one of your own animal riddles about one of the animals in the song.

Read *Bennett Cerf's Book of Animal Riddles* by Bennett Cerf or another book about animals.

Animal Riddle Four

A farm is where I make my home. I
go "oink, oink" in the mud I roam. In the shed lives a friend with
two skin - ny legs. She goes "cluck, cluck" as she lays eggs.

Animal Riddle Four

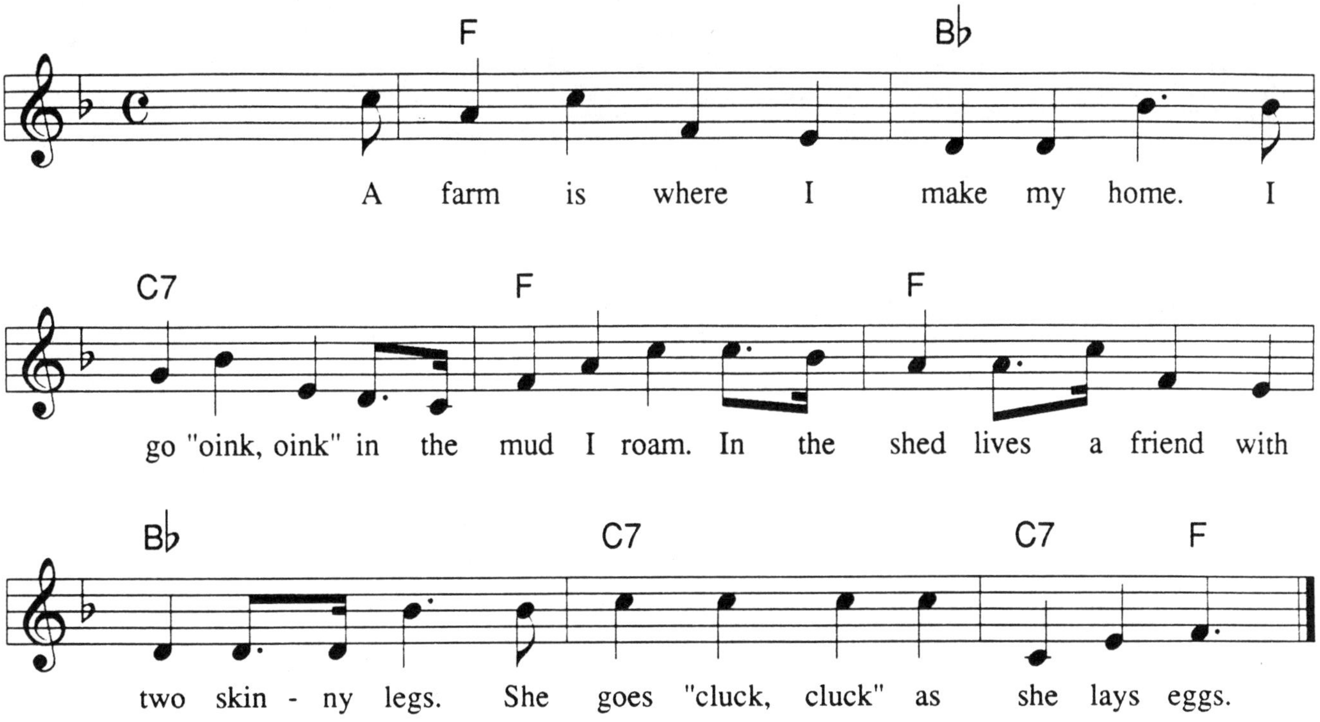
F Bb
A farm is where I make my home. I
C7 F F
go "oink, oink" in the mud I roam. In the shed lives a friend with
Bb C7 C7 F
two skin - ny legs. She goes "cluck, cluck" as she lays eggs.

WHAT ANIMALS ARE WE?

Draw and color pictures to show the answers to the riddle in the song. Write a riddle of your own about any topic. Ask others to answer your riddle.

Read *Zoodles* by Bernard Most or another book about riddles.

Apples
Ap - ples are red and yel - low and green.
Up in a tree is where they are seen.
Some - thing I like for my af - ter school treat is a
big juic - y ap - ple so yum - my and sweet.
© 1995 L. Dudley

Apples

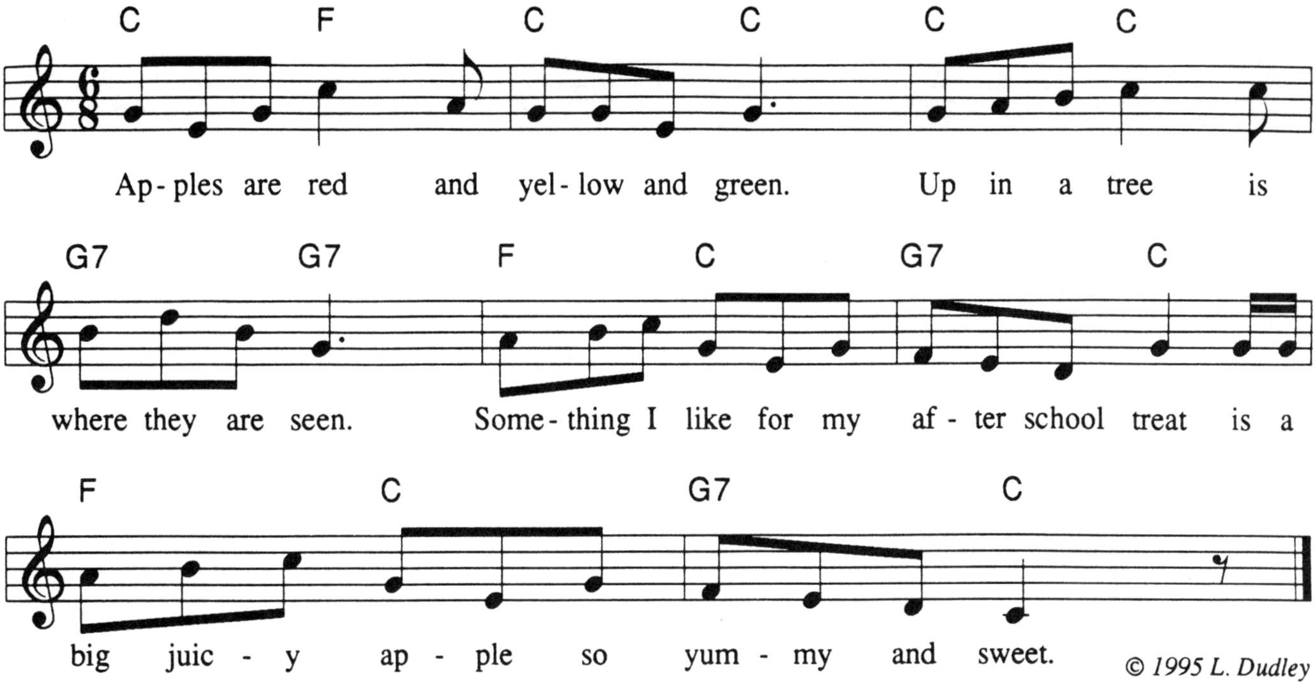

© 1995 L. Dudley

APPLE PUZZLES

1. Have a parent or teacher cut apples into halves and quarters and put each piece of apple in an individual plastic bag.

2. Place the bags in a box.

3. Without looking, each of you should take a bag from the box.

4. Find other players with apple pieces which will make a whole apple when added to your piece.

5. Discuss the fractions that make a whole apple.

6. You may eat your piece of the apple with the partner or group that put your apple puzzle together.

Read *The Seasons of Arnold's Apple Tree* by Gail Gibbons or another book about apples.

Balloons

Gently
Bal - loons, bal - loons of orange and
red. Bright blue and la - ven - der high ov - er
head. Green and yel - low, pur - ple and
pink. Pink's the one I like best, I think.
©1995 L. Dudley

Balloons

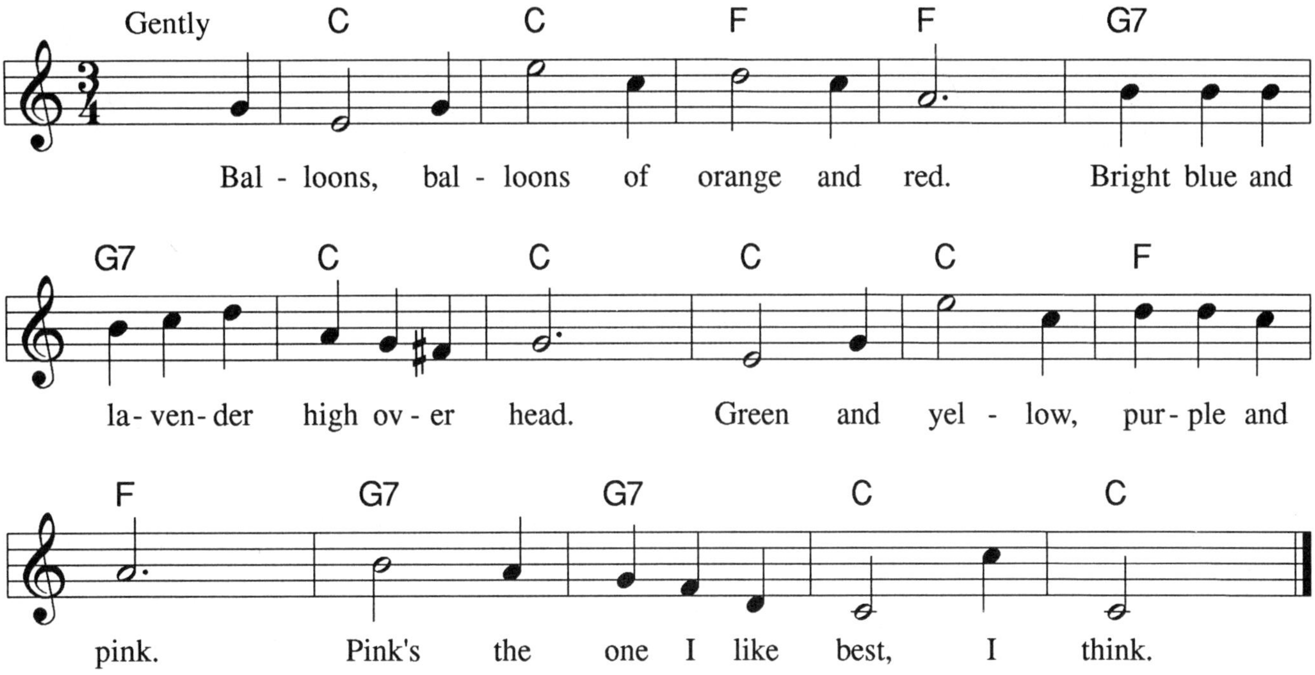

©1995 L. Dudley

ACTIVITY

Color each of the balloons the color that is printed on it. Ask an adult to spell each of the words that represent the colors. Others say the color that is spelled by the adult.

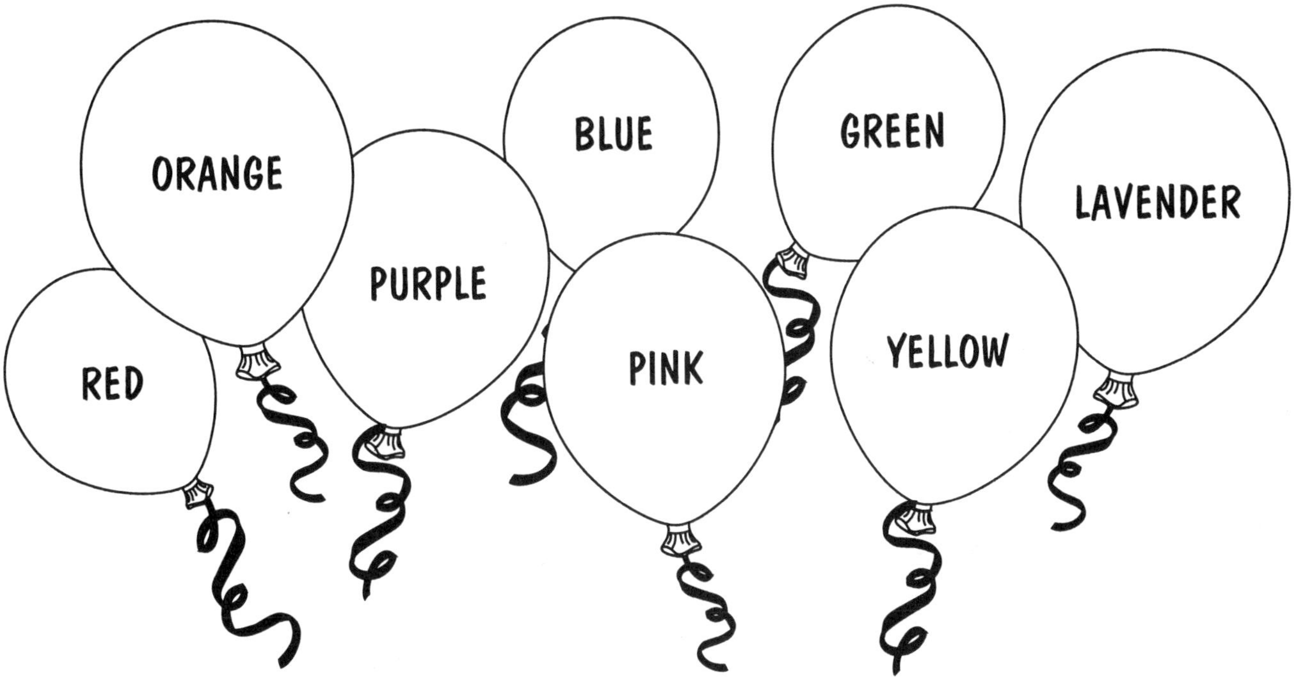

Read *The Red Balloon* by Albert Lamorisse or another book about balloons.

Bedtime

1. Ev' - ry night af - ter sup - per it's my bath time. I
2. Then I hug tight to Ed - die, he's my own bear, and
play in the bub - bles, sing a nurs' - ry rhyme. I scrub my legs, Mom
ev' - ry night he is wait - ing there. Dad reads me a book, we
wash - es my face, then off to bed - my own spe - cial place.
sing a song, and ve - ry soon, a dream comes a - long.

Bedtime

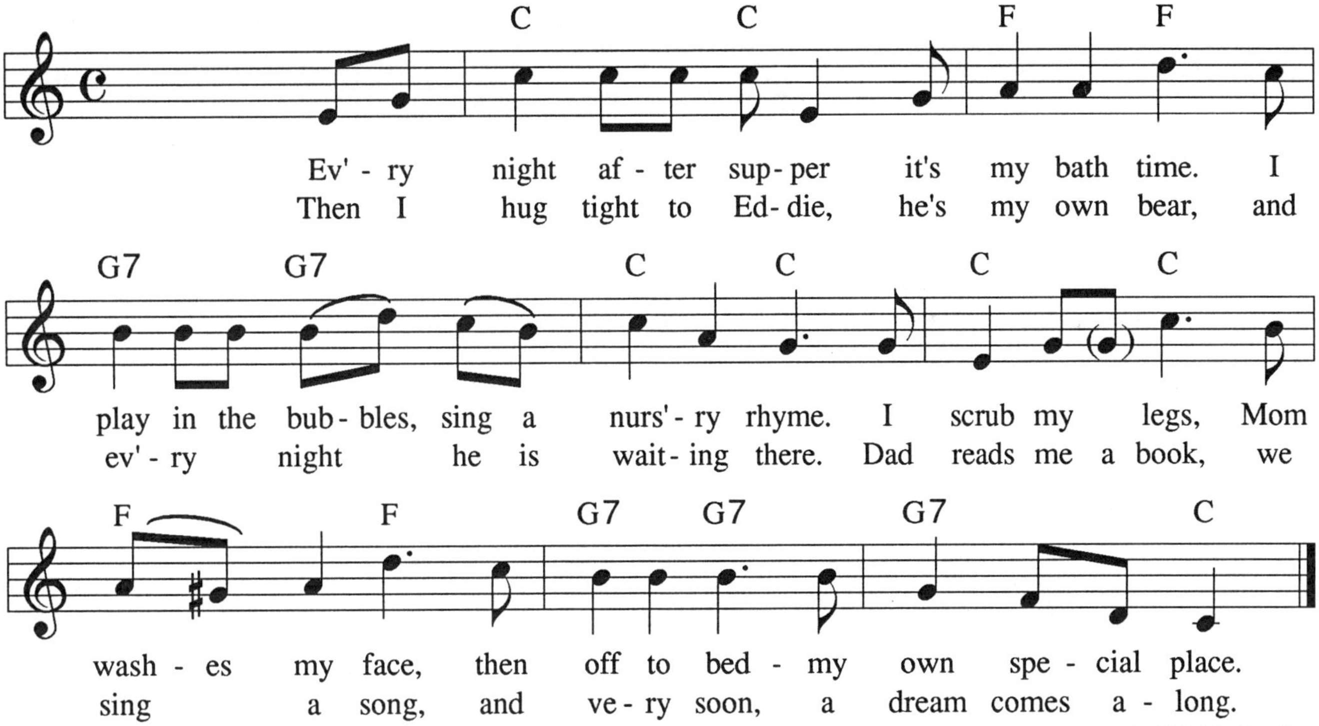
C C F F
Ev' - ry night af - ter sup - per it's my bath time. I
Then I hug tight to Ed - die, he's my own bear, and
G7 G7 C C C C
play in the bub - bles, sing a nurs' - ry rhyme. I scrub my legs, Mom
ev' - ry night he is wait - ing there. Dad reads me a book, we
F F G7 G7 G7 C
wash - es my face, then off to bed - my own spe - cial place.
sing a song, and ve - ry soon, a dream comes a - long.

© 1995 L. Dudley

ACTIVITY

Using the words from the song, write or say the pairs of words that rhyme.

____________________ ____________________

____________________ ____________________

____________________ ____________________

____________________ ____________________

Read *Ba Ba Sheep Wouldn't Go to Sleep* by Dennis Panek or another book about sleep.

Being Sick

1. My nose is run - ny, my eyes are too. My
2. I'll look at pic - tures, I'll make up a song. Mom
3. Every - one's try - ing to help me get better. Spot
head is ach - y, what can I do? "You need these pills," the
puts on mus - ic, I sing a - long. I take a nap, when I
sleeps be- side me on Dad's old sweater. I'll take my pills, I'll do
doc - tor said. "Drink lots of juice, take naps in your bed."
op - en my eyes, Dad has come home with a big sur - prise.
what I should. I think to - mor - row I'll feel good.

Being Sick

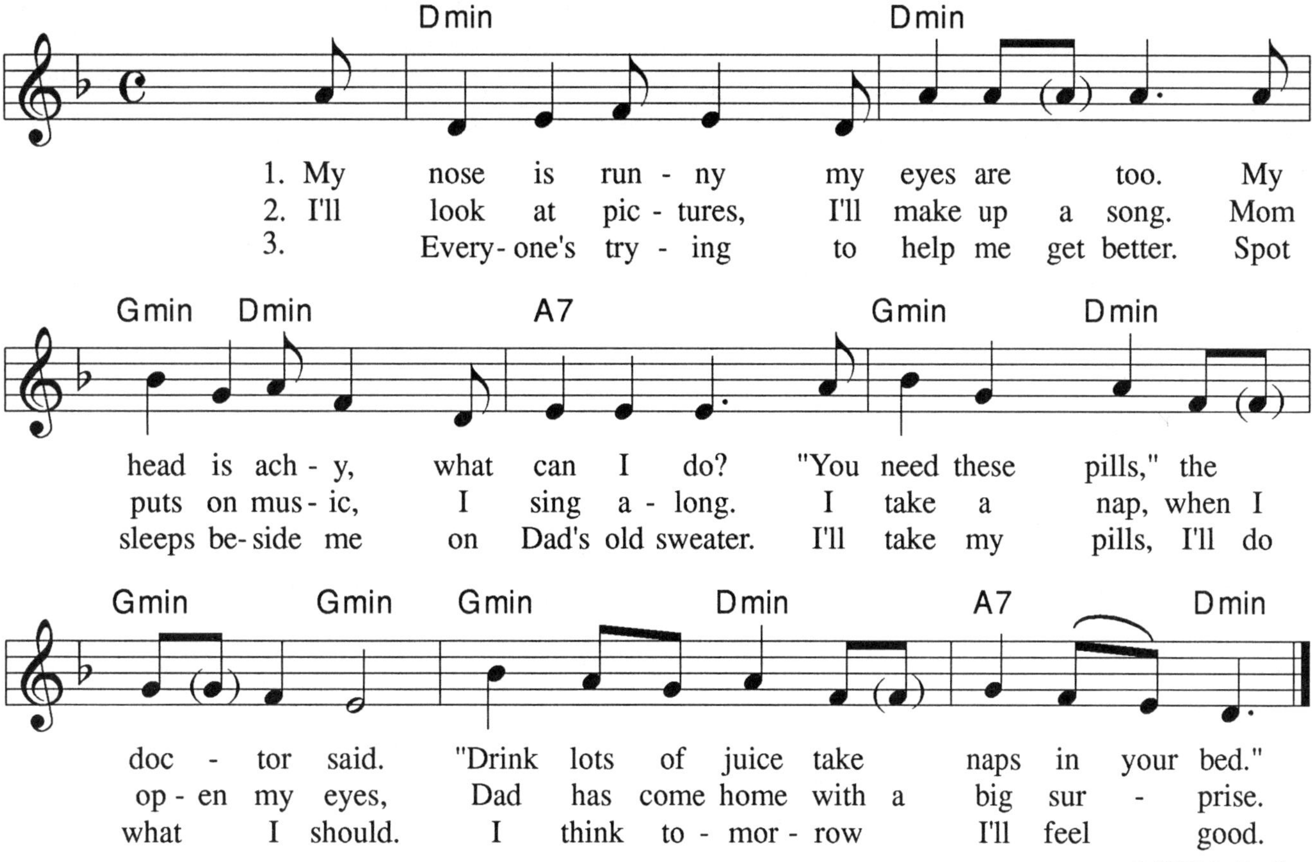
Dmin Dmin
1. My nose is run - ny my eyes are too. My
2. I'll look at pic - tures, I'll make up a song. Mom
3. Every- one's try - ing to help me get better. Spot
Gmin Dmin A7 Gmin Dmin
head is ach - y, what can I do? "You need these pills," the
puts on mus - ic, I sing a - long. I take a nap, when I
sleeps be- side me on Dad's old sweater. I'll take my pills, I'll do
Gmin Gmin Gmin Dmin A7 Dmin
doc - tor said. "Drink lots of juice take naps in your bed."
op - en my eyes, Dad has come home with a big sur - prise.
what I should. I think to - mor - row I'll feel good.

©1995 L. Dudley

ACTIVITY

Discuss what you can do to try to get well when you have a cold or flu and what you can do to try to prevent being sick. Write words that end with the same sound as in the word 'sick' and in the word 'well.' This can include proper names.

SICK	WELL
____________________	____________________
____________________	____________________
____________________	____________________
____________________	____________________
____________________	____________________

Read *The Sick-in-Bed Birthday* by Linda Wagner Tyler or another book about being sick.

Breakfast

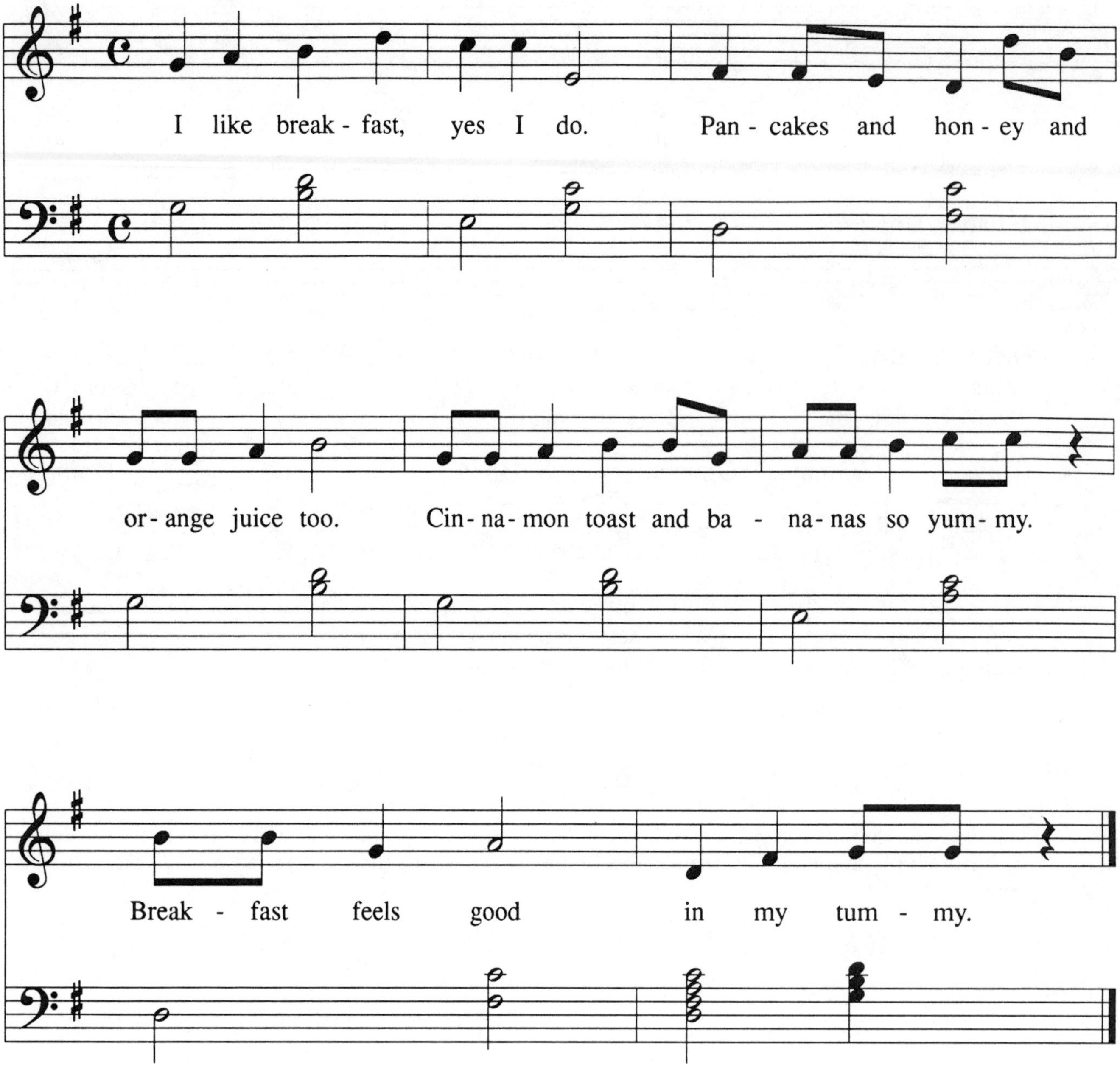
I like break - fast, yes I do. Pan - cakes and hon - ey and
or- ange juice too. Cin- na- mon toast and ba - na- nas so yum- my.
Break - fast feels good in my tum - my.

©1995 L.Dudley

Breakfast

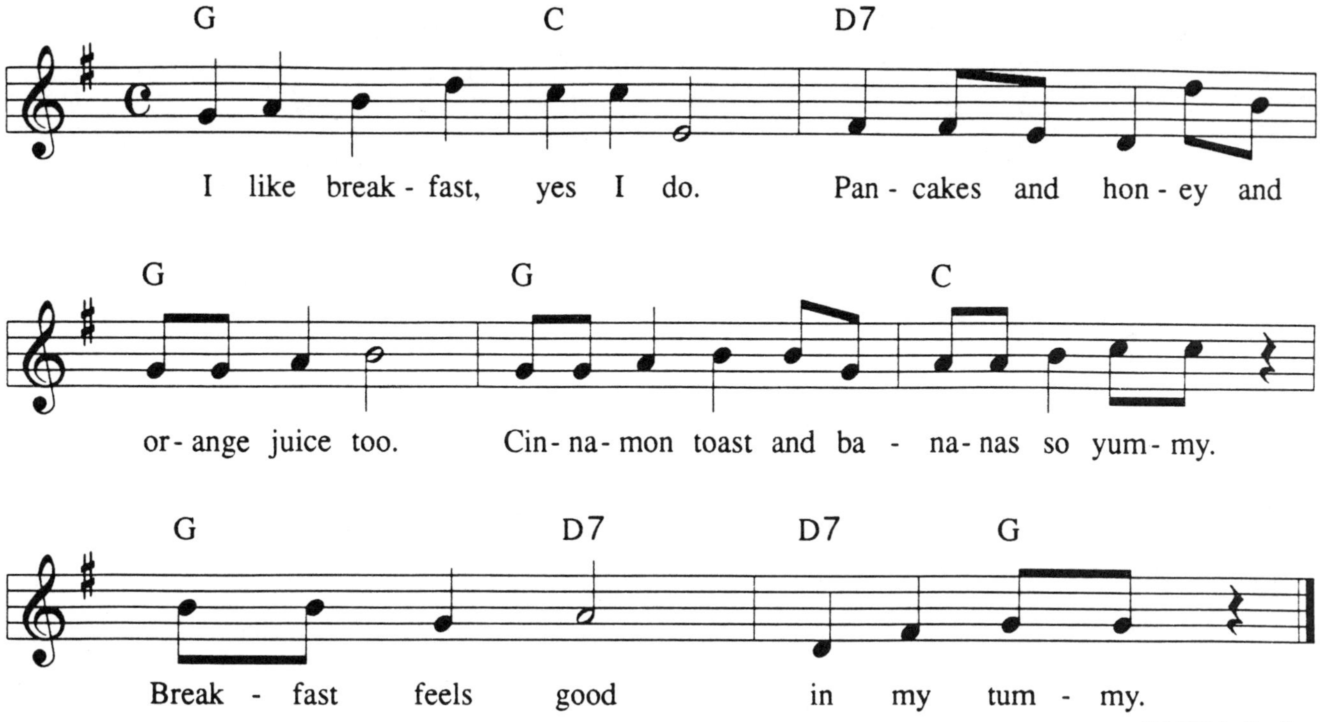
G C D7
I like break - fast, yes I do. Pan - cakes and hon - ey and
G G C
or- ange juice too. Cin- na- mon toast and ba - na- nas so yum- my.
G D7 D7 G
Break - fast feels good in my tum - my.

©1995 L.Dudley

ACTIVITY

Discuss the food pyramid below. Draw and cut out various kinds of food for a nutritious meal. Glue the paper food to a paper plate. Discuss why you chose each kind of food on your plate.

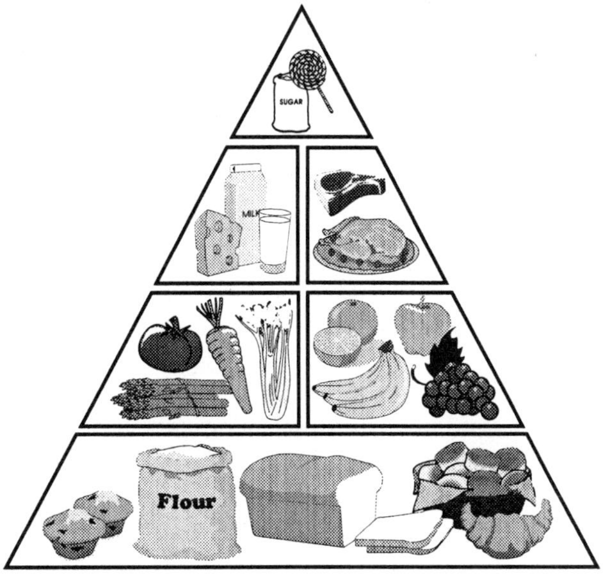

Read *Mel's Diner* by Marissa Moss or another book about meals.

Bubbles

A hand drum or rhythm sticks may be played on ❉

Bub - bles in my bath, and bub - bles I can blow.
LH over
LH over
Bub - bles all a - round, float - ing up they go. I blow bub-bles, now they go
LH over
LH over
❉
float-ing past, but the sad thing 'bout my bub - bles is they ne-ver last. POP!
LH over

©1995 L. Dudley

Bubbles

A hand drum or rhythm sticks may be played on ❉

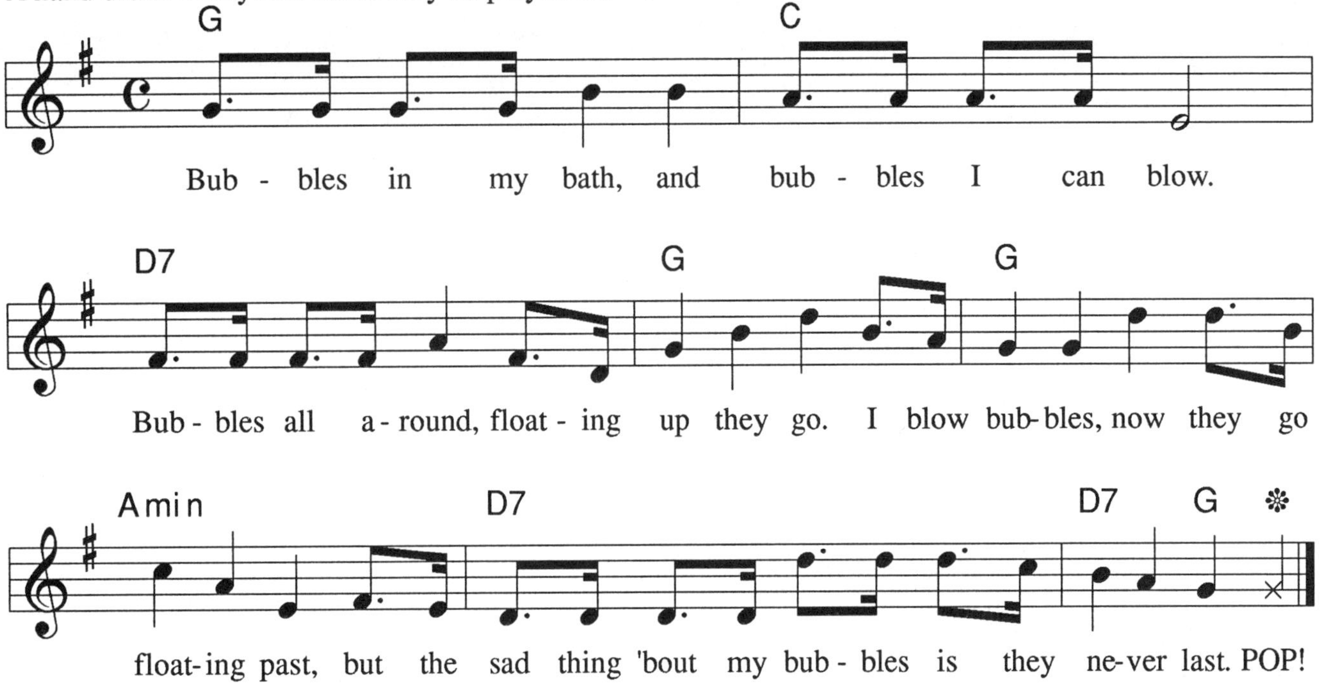
G C
Bub - bles in my bath, and bub - bles I can blow.
D7 G G
Bub - bles all a - round, float - ing up they go. I blow bub-bles, now they go
Amin D7 D7 G ❉
float-ing past, but the sad thing 'bout my bub - bles is they ne-ver last. POP!

©1995 L. Dudley

SOAP BUBBLE RECIPE

1/2 cup of water

2 tablespoons of liquid soap

Mix the water and soap together in a paper cup with a straw.

Make the recipe above. Dip a straw in the bubble soap and blow bubbles with it. Place the straw in your mouth after you have dipped it in the soap mixture. As you pop each of the bubbles, spell the word 'B-U-B-B-L-E' by saying one letter on each pop. Also count the bubbles by 1's and by sets.

Read *Soap Bubble Magic* by Seymour Simon or another book about bubbles.

A Builder

X-sticks pattern throughout the song.
Instruments may be played on ❉
I'd like to be a build - er, of
I'll wear a hard hat, heavy gloves, and
hous - es and of schools, of play - grounds, malls and of - fi - ces, of
work boots on my feet, a spe - cial vest for safe - ty when I'm
streets and swim - ming pools. Then I will saw, saw, saw, and I'll go
work - ing on the street.
tap, tap, tap. E - lec - tric tools will whirr, and they'll go zap, zap, zap.

A Builder

Instruments may be played on ❁

F C7
1. I'd like to be a build - er, of
2. I'll wear a hard hat, heavy gloves, and
F F B♭ Gm
hous - es and of schools, of play - grounds, malls and of - fi - ces, of
work boots on my feet, a spe - cial vest for safe - ty when I'm
C7 F F F F
streets and swim - ming pools. Then I will saw, saw, saw, and I'll go
work - ing on the street.
B♭ B♭ B♭ C7 C7 C7 F B♭ F
tap, tap, tap. E - lec - tric tools will whirr, and they'll go zap, zap, zap.

©1995 L. Dudley

ACTIVITY

Use toy blocks to make buildings of various heights. Measure and record the height of each building.

Building 1: ______________________________

Building 2: ______________________________

Building 3: ______________________________

Read *Building a Bridge* by Lisa Shook Begaye or another book about building.

A Busy Old Worm

A Busy Old Worm

C F C G7 C D7 G
I know a-bout some-one who loves to eat dirt, and if it rains she doesn't get hurt. A
C F C G7 C G7
tun-nel's her home, she digs ev'-ry day. Dig-ging for her is not work, it is play.
C F G7 C G7 G7
And she goes down, down, down in the ground. She goes so far she may
C C C F G7 C G7 G7 G7 C
nev-er be found. Dig, dig, wig-gle and squirm. This is the life for a hap-py old worm.

ACTIVITY

Use a ruler to draw a 1 inch worm, a 2 inch worm, and a 3 inch worm in the boxes below.

Read *A Worm Tale* by Barbara Lindren or another book about worms.

Butterflies

Finger cymbals may be played on ❉

But - ter - flies are orange and black and some- times pur - ple too. One
Piano 8va throughout
sits up- on a rose bush, it's wings are ver - y blue. They
flut- ter a- round our flow - ers, they fly up in the sky. Per-
❉
haps we should have a new name, and call them flut - ter - bys.

Butterflies

Finger cymbals may be played on ❊

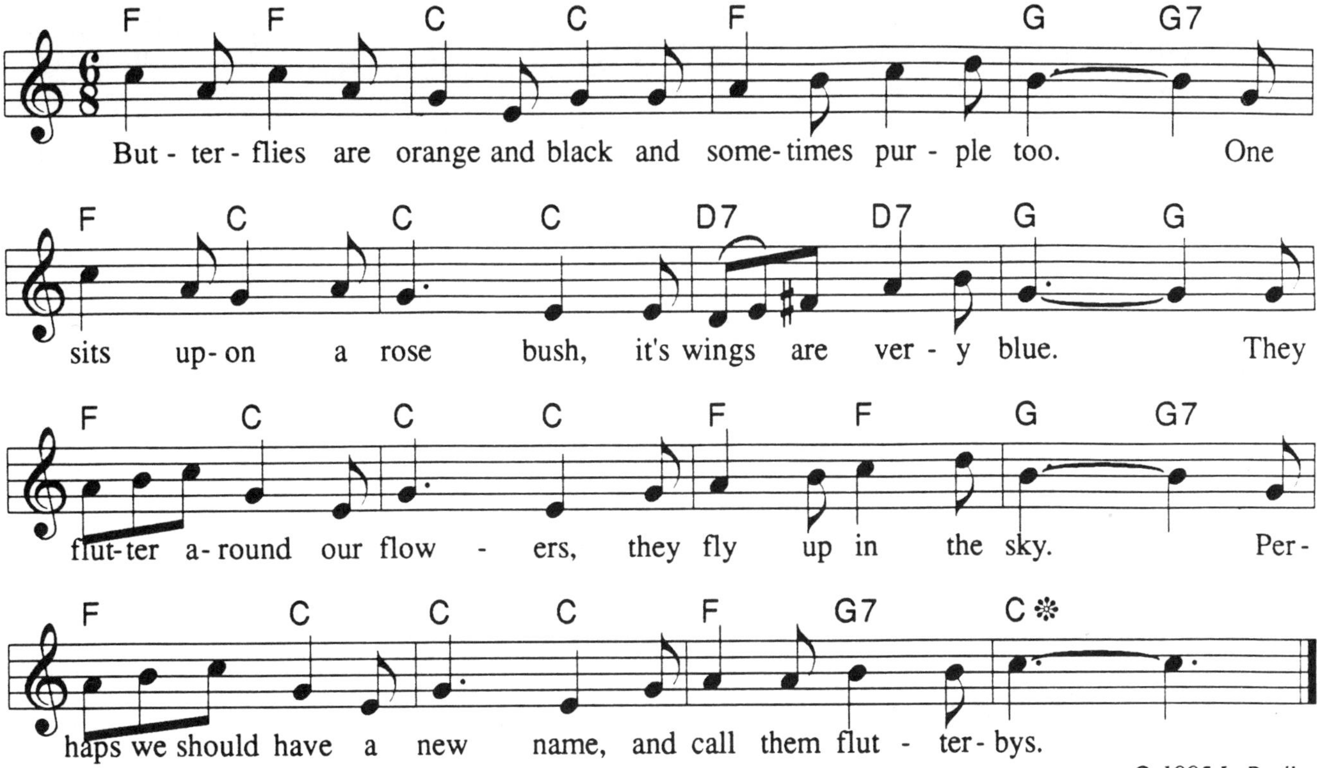
F F C C F G G7
But - ter - flies are orange and black and some- times pur - ple too. One
F C C C D7 D7 G G
sits up- on a rose bush, it's wings are ver - y blue. They
F C C C F F G G7
flut- ter a- round our flow - ers, they fly up in the sky. Per-
F C C C F G7 C ❊
haps we should have a new name, and call them flut - ter- bys.

ACTIVITY

Observe pictures from posters and books of various kinds of butterflies from countries around the world. Draw, label and color a butterfly from one or more of the countries. Tape each butterfly on the proper country on a world map that is on a bulletin board.

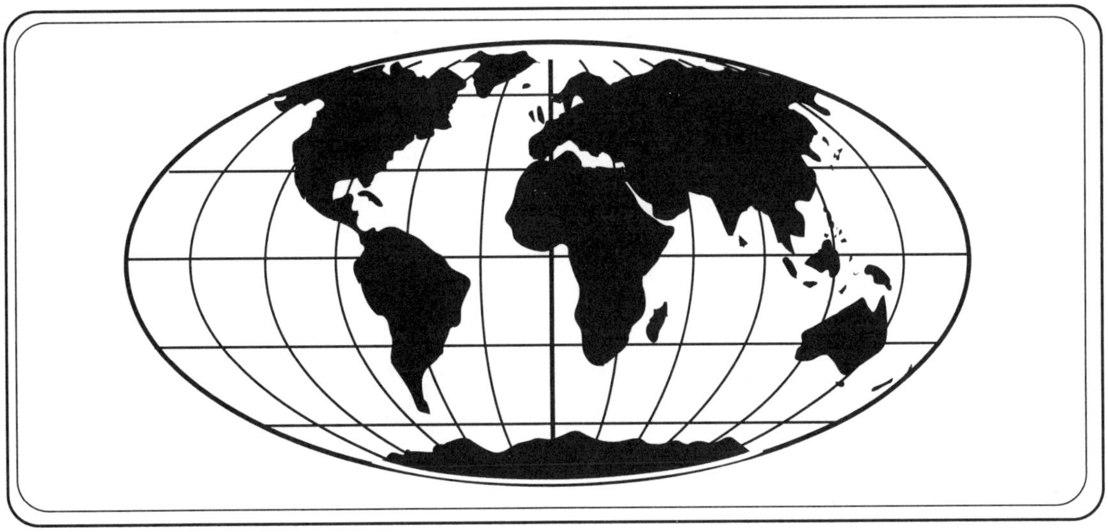

Read the article "Butterfly" in *The World Book Encyclopedia* or another encyclopedia, or read a book about butterflies.

The Circus

Introduction
8va
We went to the cir - cus when it came to town. There was a par-ade, I shook
hands with a clown. The ti - gers jumped through great big hoops, the
pon - ies ran in a ring. A la - dy sat on an
el - e - phant's head, and high in the air was a swing.

The Circus

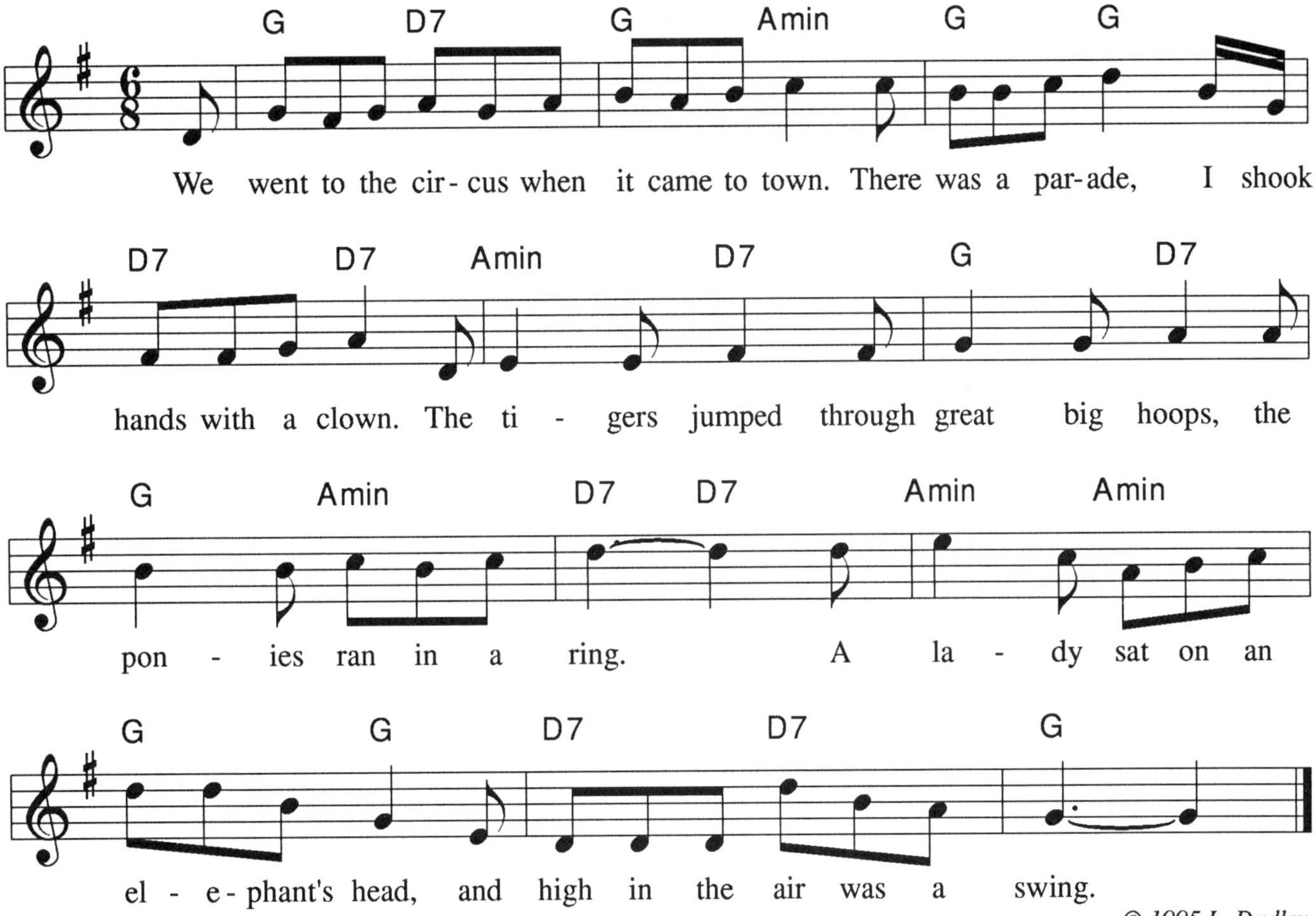
G D7 G Amin G G
We went to the cir- cus when it came to town. There was a par-ade, I shook
D7 D7 Amin D7 G D7
hands with a clown. The ti - gers jumped through great big hoops, the
G Amin D7 D7 Amin Amin
pon - ies ran in a ring. A la - dy sat on an
G G D7 D7 G
el - e- phant's head, and high in the air was a swing.

© 1995 L. Dudley

ACTIVITY

Measure and cut off a yard of adding machine tape. Draw and color a circus parade on it. Glue the ends of the paper together to make a standing ring.

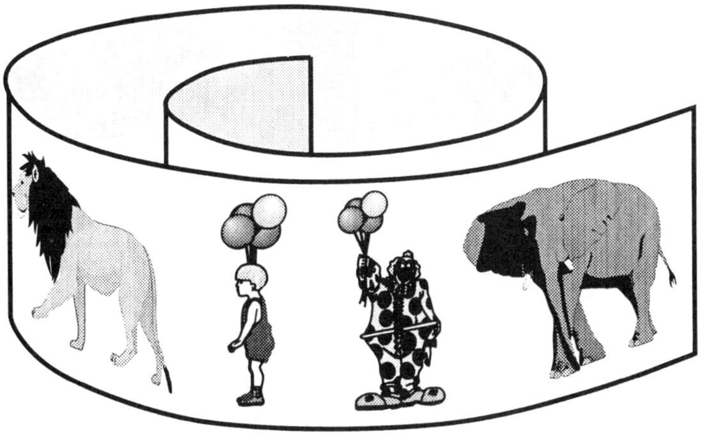

Read *Peter Spier's Circus!* by Peter Spier or another book about a circus.

The Counting Song

1. I see the sun and an ap - ple tree. The
2. Two ap - ples grew on a branch of the tree.
3. Buzz, buzz - ing bees, count them one, two, three.
4. Four blue - birds high in the sky do I see.
5. Five flow - ers sway - ing so hap - pi - ly.
sun shines down on the tree and me.

©1995 L. Dudley

The Counting Song

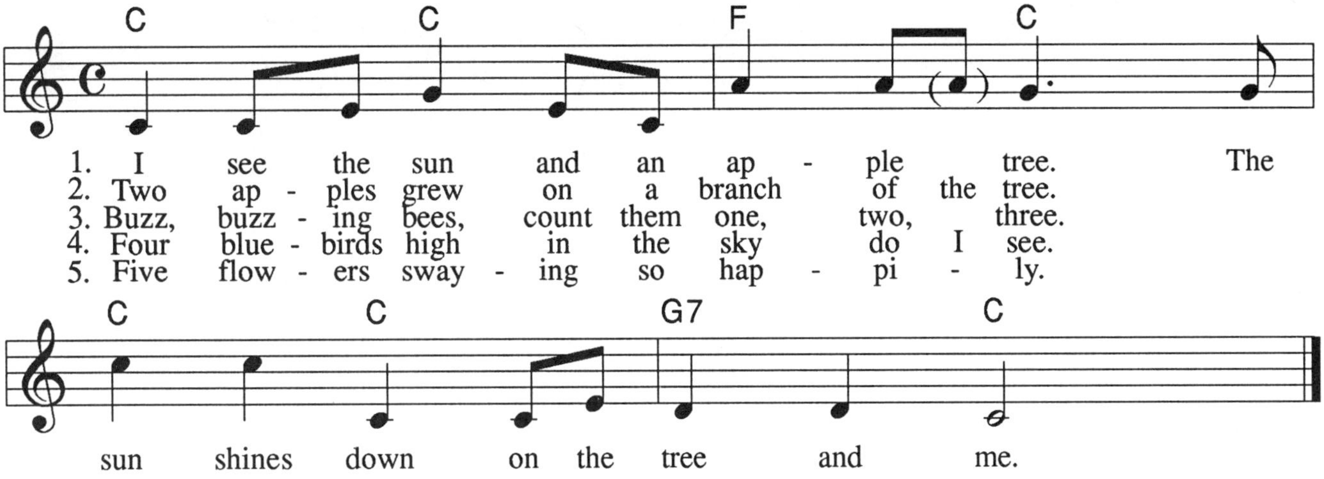
C C F C C C G7 C
1. I see the sun and an ap - ple tree. The
2. Two ap - ples grew on a branch of the tree.
3. Buzz, buzz - ing bees, count them one, two, three.
4. Four blue - birds high in the sky do I see.
5. Five flow - ers sway - ing so hap - pi - ly.
sun shines down on the tree and me.

ACTIVITY

Discuss the sets of objects in the song. Draw and color a picture with the various sets of objects. Check to see that you have equal amounts of sets in your picture as are in the song.

Read *Each Orange Had 8 Slices* by Paul Giganti, Jr. or another counting book.

The Farm

© 1995 L. Dudley

The Farm

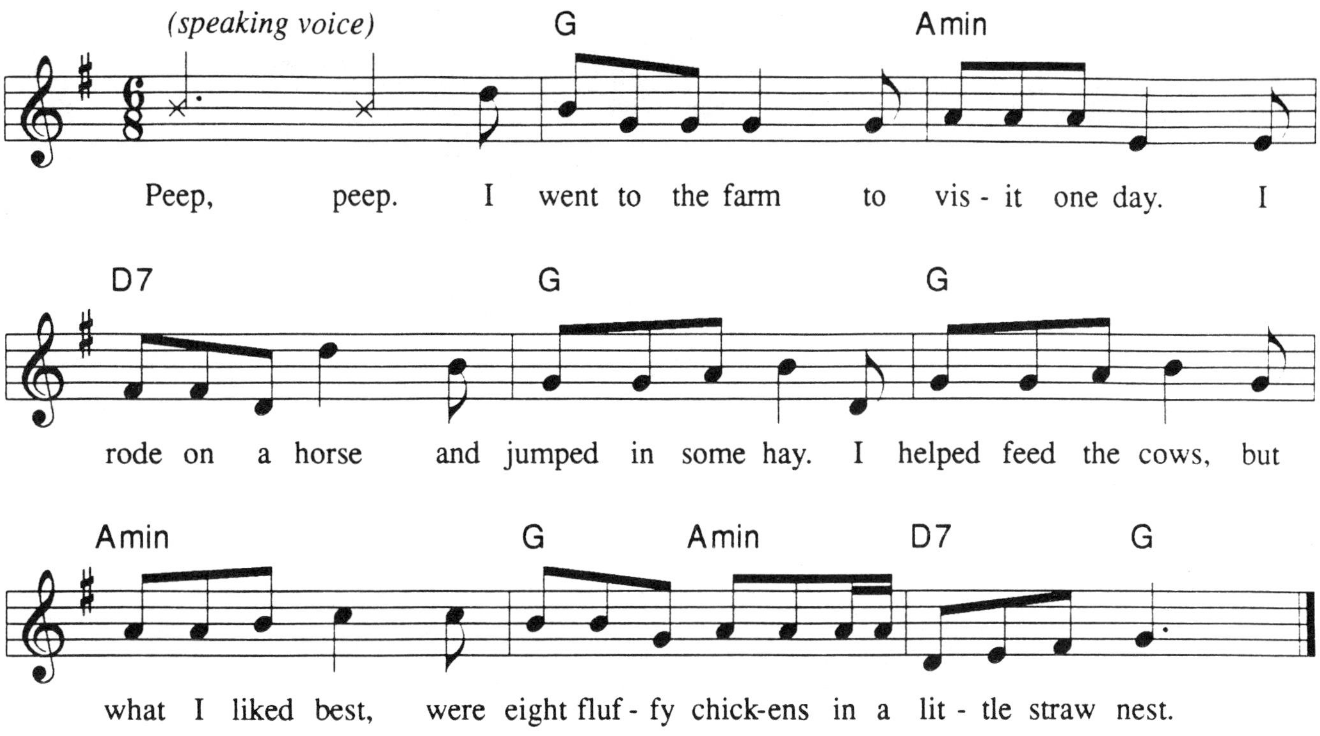
(speaking voice)
G
Amin
Peep, peep. I went to the farm to vis - it one day. I
D7
G
G
rode on a horse and jumped in some hay. I helped feed the cows, but
Amin
G
Amin
D7
G
what I liked best, were eight fluf - fy chick-ens in a lit - tle straw nest.

© 1995 L. Dudley

ACTIVITY

Draw the same number of chickens in the nest as mentioned in the song. There are __________chickens in the song and there are_________chickens in your picture. Write or tell some story problems about the chickens in your picture.

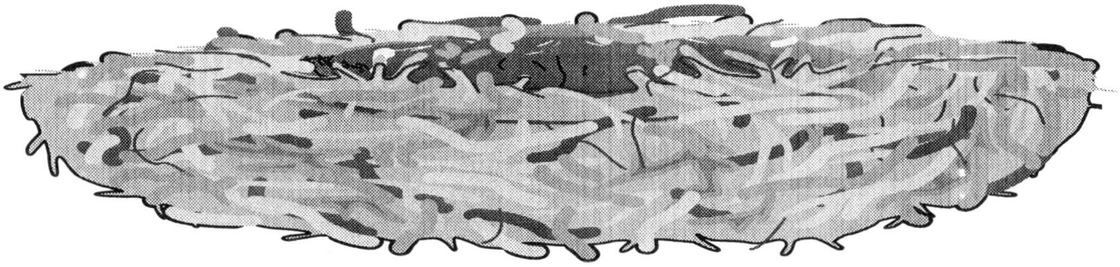

Read *Farm Morning* by David McPhail or another book about a farm.

Five Little Bunnies

Hop, hop, hop, hop. 1. Five lit - tle bun - nies, in the grass so tall.
2. Four lit - tle bun - nies, that no one can see.
3. Three lit - tle bun - nies, eat - ing ten - der clover.
4. Two lit - tle bun - nies, sit - ting in the sun.
5. One lit - tle bun - ny, went to find some fun.
One went ex - plor - ing, now there are four in all.
One hopped a - way, and now there are three.
One was scared a - way by a big dog named Rov - er.
One heard a noise, now there is one.
How man - y bun - nies? Now there are none.

©1995 L. Dudley

Five Little Bunnies

1. Five lit - tle bun - nies, in the grass so tall.
2. Four lit - tle bun - nies, that no one can see.
3. Three lit - tle bun - nies, eat - ing ten - der clover.
4. Two lit - tle bun - nies, sit - ting in the sun.
5. One lit - tle bun - ny, went to find some fun.

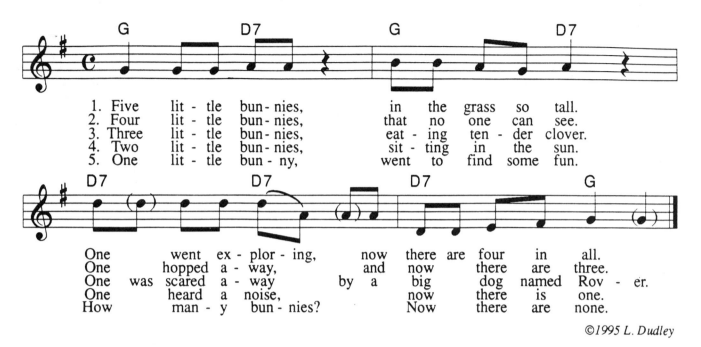

One went ex - plor - ing, now there are four in all.
One hopped a - way, and now there are three.
One was scared a - way by a big dog named Rov - er.
One heard a noise, now there is one.
How man - y bun - nies? Now there are none.

©1995 L. Dudley

ACTIVITY

Write math story problems so that the answers are "Five Bunnies."

_____ bunnies + _____ bunnies = _____5_____

_____ bunnies + _____ bunnies = _____5_____

_____ bunnies + _____ bunnies = _____5_____

_____ bunnies - _____1_____ bunnies = _____

_____ bunnies - _____5_____ bunnies = _____

_____ bunnies - _____0_____ bunnies = _____

 Read *Bunches and Bunches of Bunnies* by Louise Mathews or another book about bunnies.

From *Songs to Sing and Picture*. Activities © 1996 Harriet R. Kinghorn. Teacher Ideas Press. (800) 237-6124. Music © 1995 Lillian L. Dudley.

The Five Senses

My eyes can see a rose or a tree, my ears can hear a bum-ble-bee, I
smell a piz- za with my nose, I feel the sand with my fin- gers and toes. I
feel, I smell, I see, I hear, I use fin- gers, nose and eyes and ears. We can
al- so learn by a taste test, and some- times that's the way I like the best.

©1995 L. Dudley

The Five Senses

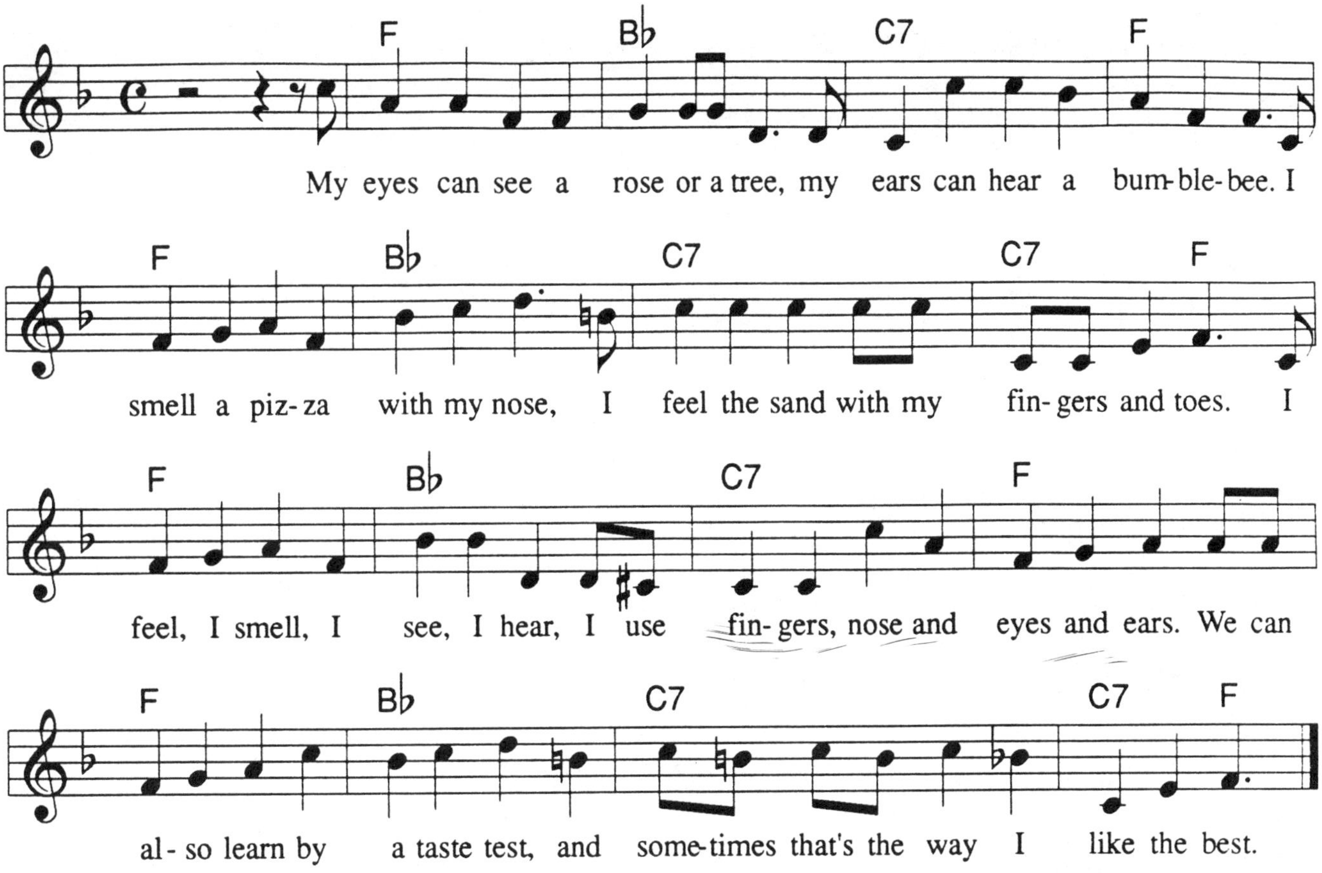
F Bb C7 F
My eyes can see a rose or a tree, my ears can hear a bum-ble-bee. I
F Bb C7 C7 F
smell a piz-za with my nose, I feel the sand with my fin-gers and toes. I
F Bb C7 F
feel, I smell, I see, I hear, I use fin-gers, nose and eyes and ears. We can
F Bb C7 C7 F
al-so learn by a taste test, and some-times that's the way I like the best.

©1995 L. Dudley

ACTIVITY

Complete the sentences below.

I like to see ______________________________

I like to hear ______________________________

I like to smell ______________________________

I like to taste ______________________________

I like to touch ______________________________

Read *My Five Senses* by Aliki or another book about senses.

Friends Around the World

Tambourines may be played on ❉

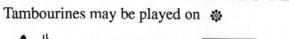

©1995 L. Dudley

Friends Around the World

Tambourines may be played on ❊

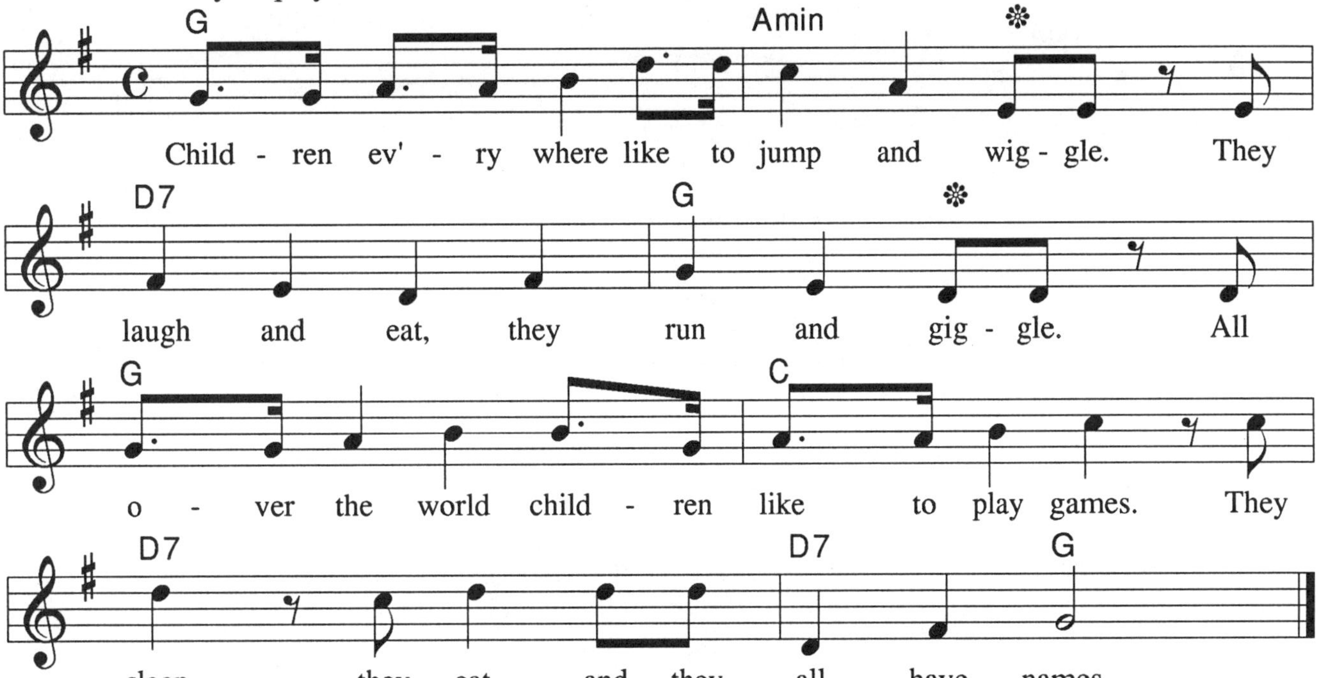

©1995 L. Dudley

ACTIVITY

1. Find and read books about games that children play around the world such as the one listed below.
2. Play some of the games that you learn about from your readings.

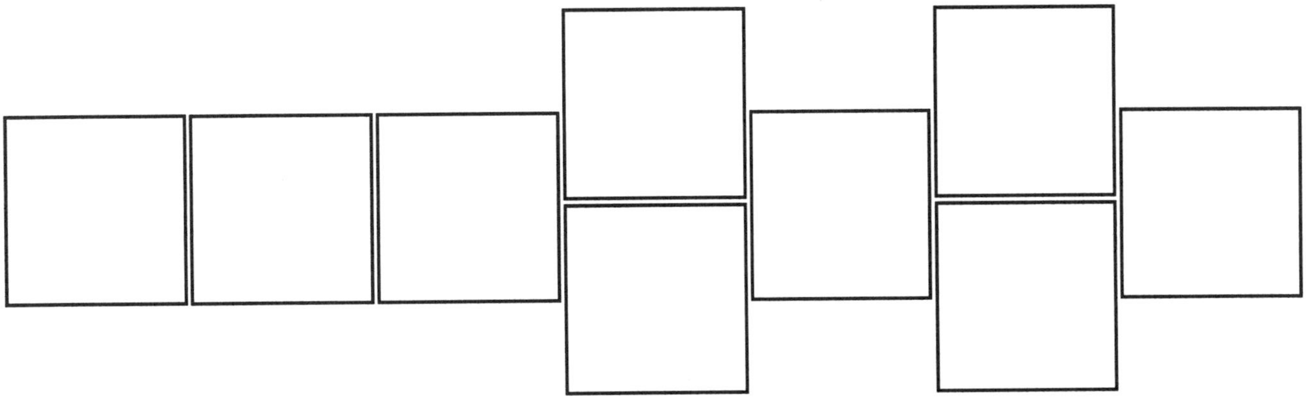

Read *Hopscotch Around the World* by Mary D. Lankford.

Grandma

Introduction
1.Grand- ma gives kiss - es, and lis- tens to wish- es.
2.Grand- ma reads books and puts worms on the hooks.
Grand-ma gives hugs, and looks at my bugs. And when we go shop- ping, she
Grand-ma plays cards and works out in our yards. When it's time for my nap, I crawl
does - n't mind stop- ping. She cooks me spa- ghet- ti and ap - ple brown bet- ty.
in - to her lap. She sings me a song, and I sing a - long.

©1995 L. Dudley

Grandma

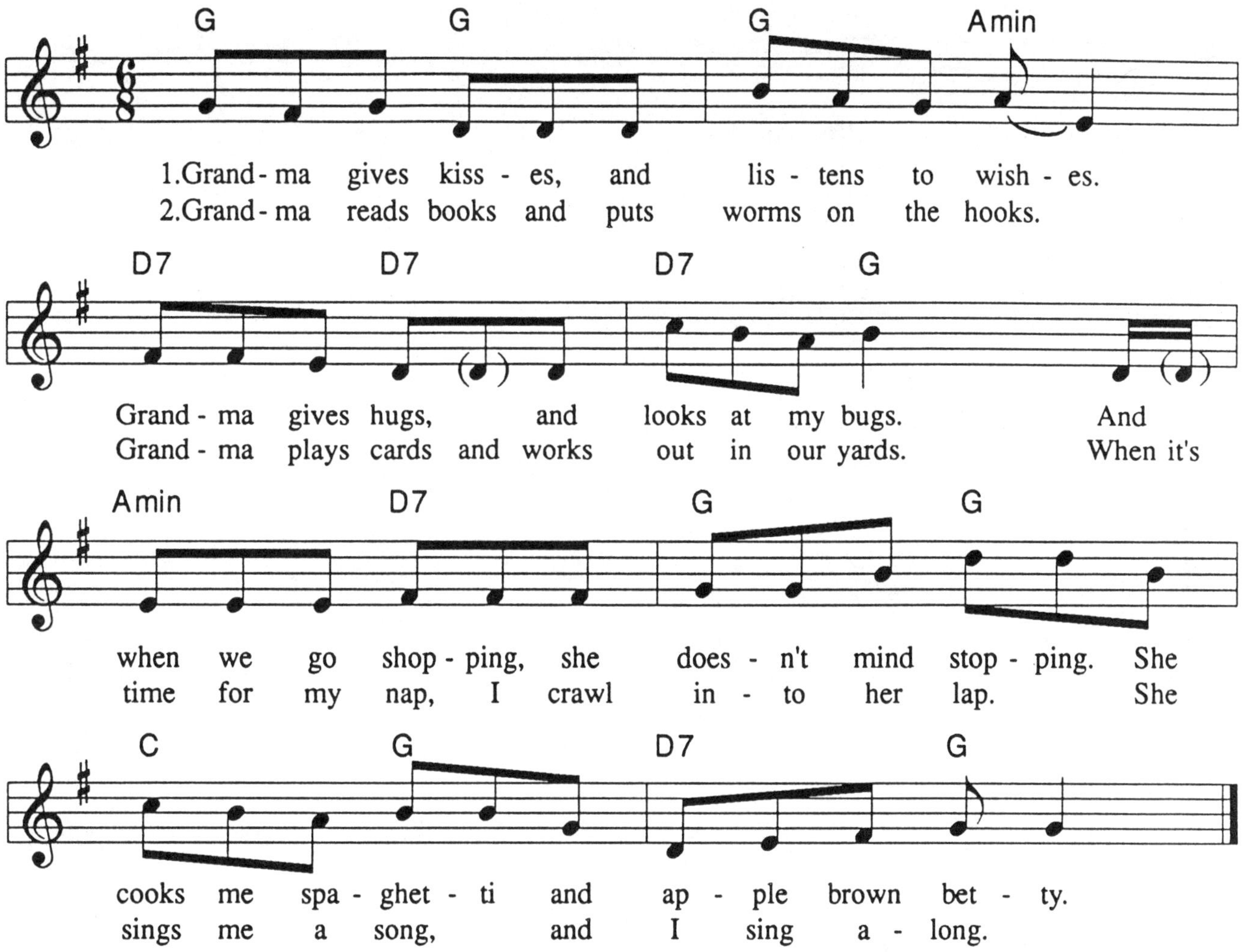
G G G Amin
1.Grand-ma gives kiss-es, and lis-tens to wish-es.
2.Grand-ma reads books and puts worms on the hooks.
D7 D7 D7 G
Grand-ma gives hugs, and looks at my bugs. And
Grand-ma plays cards and works out in our yards. When it's
Amin D7 G G
when we go shop-ping, she does-n't mind stop-ping. She
time for my nap, I crawl in-to her lap. She
C G D7 G
cooks me spa-ghet-ti and ap-ple brown bet-ty.
sings me a song, and I sing a-long.

©1995 L. Dudley

ACTIVITY

Draw a picture of the child and the grandmother in the song doing something together, or draw something that you and your grandmother like to do together.

Read *Once upon a Time and Grandma* by Lenore Blegvad or another book about a grandma.

Grandpa

I'm go - ing to have a ve - ry spe - cial day, 'cause
Grand - pa's com - ing to get me, and we're leav - ing right a - way. I
packed a bag, 'cause I get to stay, and they have some spe - cial
games we will play. Oh, I'm as hap - py as I can be, 'cause
I love Grand - pa, and he loves me. When we get there, I'll
get a big hug, and Grand - ma will say I'm her lit - tle bug.

Grandpa

G G
I'm go - ing to have a ve - ry spe - cial day, 'cause
C D7
Grand- pa's com- ing to get me, and we're leav - ing right a - way. I
G C G D7
packed a bag, 'cause I get to stay, and they have some spe - cial
D7 G G Amin
games we will play. Oh, I'm as hap- py as I can be, 'cause
D7 G G
I love Grand - pa, and he loves me. When we get there, I'll
C D7 G
get a big hug, and Grand - ma will say I'm her lit - tle bug.

©1995 L. Dudley

ACTIVITY

On another sheet of paper draw and color a picture about the song, or draw a picture about something that you and your grandfather like to do together.

 Read *Could Be Worse* by James Stevenson or another book about a grandpa.

Happiness

Jump, jump, jump for joy. Let's be hap - py ev' - ry
girl and boy. Stamp your feet, now stretch ver - y high,
with both hands try to touch the sky. So wig - gle and wag - gle and
turn a - round, clap your hands, make a hap - py sound. (CLAP)

Happiness

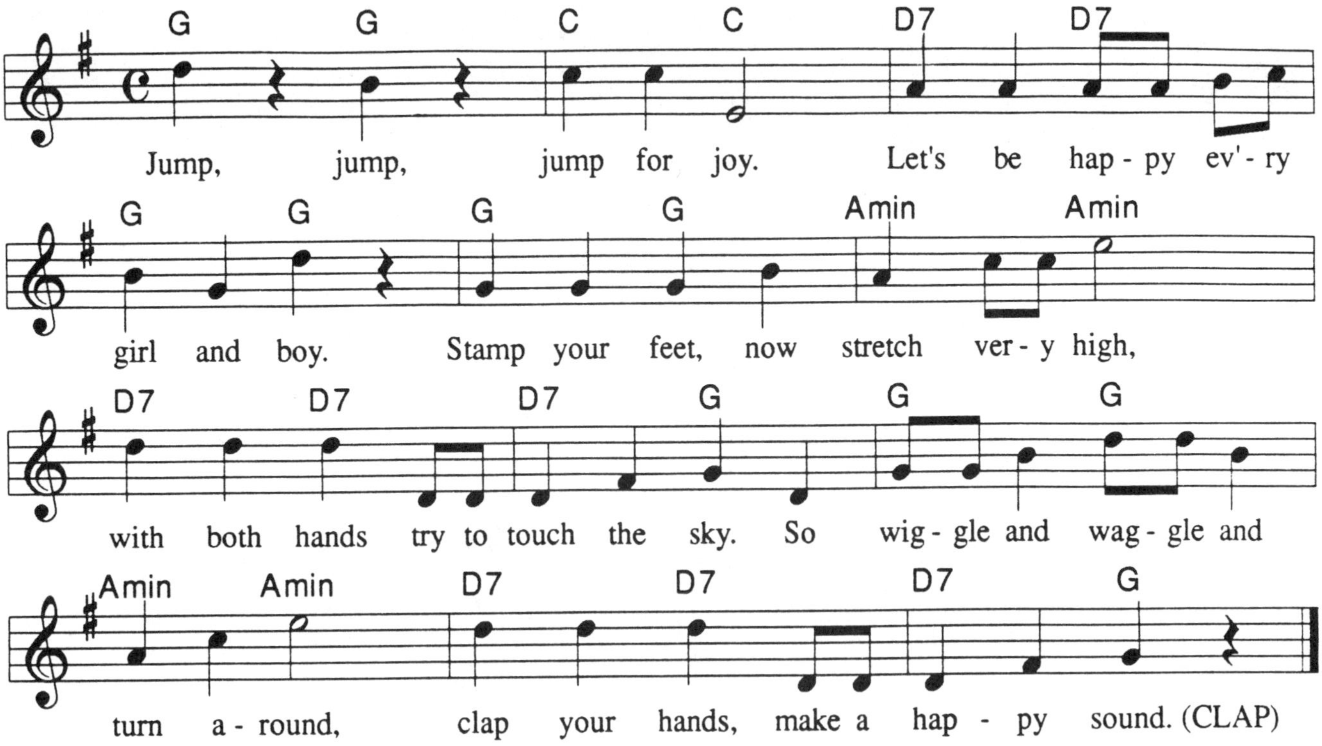
G G C C D7 D7
Jump, jump, jump for joy. Let's be hap - py ev'- ry
G G G G Amin Amin
girl and boy. Stamp your feet, now stretch ver - y high,
D7 D7 D7 G G G
with both hands try to touch the sky. So wig - gle and wag - gle and
Amin Amin D7 D7 D7 G
turn a - round, clap your hands, make a hap - py sound. (CLAP)

©1995 L. Dudley

ACTIVITY

Write an acrostic poem with the letters in the word 'Happiness.' Write or say a word that tells how you are happy using each letter.

H ______________________________

A ______________________________

P ______________________________

P ______________________________

I ______________________________

N ______________________________

E ______________________________

S ______________________________

S ______________________________

Read *Feelings: Happy* by Janine Amos or another book about happiness.

Hats

©1995 L. Dudley

Hats

Lively
F C7 F F C7
Hats, hats, hats. What won - der - ful things are hats.
F B♭ F C7 F Fine
They can be fun or to keep off the sun. Hats, hats, hats.
F B♭ C7
1. A hat may have a bill in front, and then it's called a
2. A hat must tie and stay on tight for peop - le who keep
F B♭ C7 1. F B♭ C7 F
cap. Some hats are hard for safe - ty's sake, and fas - ten with a strap.
bees. You wear a warm hat
2. F B♭ C7 F D.C. al Fine
when it's cold, so ears and neck won't freeze.
©1995 L. Dudley

ACTIVITY

Draw and color a picture of yourself wearing one of the hats in the song. Tell others about your picture, including why you chose this hat to wear in your picture.

Read *Martin's Hats* by Joan W. Blos or another book about hats.

Healthy Snacks

1. I'm hun - gry, I'm hun - gry, and I want to eat.
2. An ap - ple, graham crac - kers, I'll drink some co - coa.
3. I've got it, I've got it, and it will taste great. Let's
I'll go ask Mom for a nice tast - y treat. "A
Orange and pear slic - es are tast - y, I know. Some
get out a cup and my ted - dy bear plate. To
snack," says my Moth - er, "now choose a sur - prise.
rai - sins, a car - rot and cel - e - ry sticks. And
drink I'd like cran - ap - ple juice, if you please. And
One that will be ve - ry health - y and wise."
if I choose orange juice, then I will help mix.
for my good snack, I choose crack - ers and cheese.

Healthy Snacks

©1995 L. Dudley

ACTIVITY

Discuss various kinds of healthy food that can be eaten as snacks. Draw and illustrate a booklet of nutritious snacks. This can be an individual or group project.

Read *Healthy Food Train* by Jane B. Moncure or another book about healthy snacks.

Holidays

©1995 L. Dudley

Holidays

G Amin D7 G
A hol- i- day is a spe-cial day, and a spe- cial day can be a hol- i- day. In the
G Amin D7 G
month of ___ there's a hol - i - day; _______ is this hol - i - day. With
G Amin D7 G
__________ we will dec - or - ate, as ______ (Day) we cel - e - brate.
(Time)
E7 Amin D7 G
May-be we will dance in a ring, and spe - cial songs for this time we'll sing.

©1995 L. Dudley

ACTIVITY

Take turns saying a few words and phrases that remind you of the holiday. Draw small pictures in the frame below to make a collage of 'Holiday Memories.'

Read the books in a holiday series by Edna Barth or another book about holidays.

I Like Orange

Introduction
1. Orange is my fav - 'rite col - or, and
2. Orange juice and peach - es, can - ta - loupe,
I will tell you why. Good things to eat like
cheddar cheese, apri - cot jam. Butter - nut squash and
car - rots are orange, and so is pump - kin for a pie.
cream - y cheese sauce, and sweet po - ta - toes cooked with ham.

©1995 L. Dudley

I Like Orange

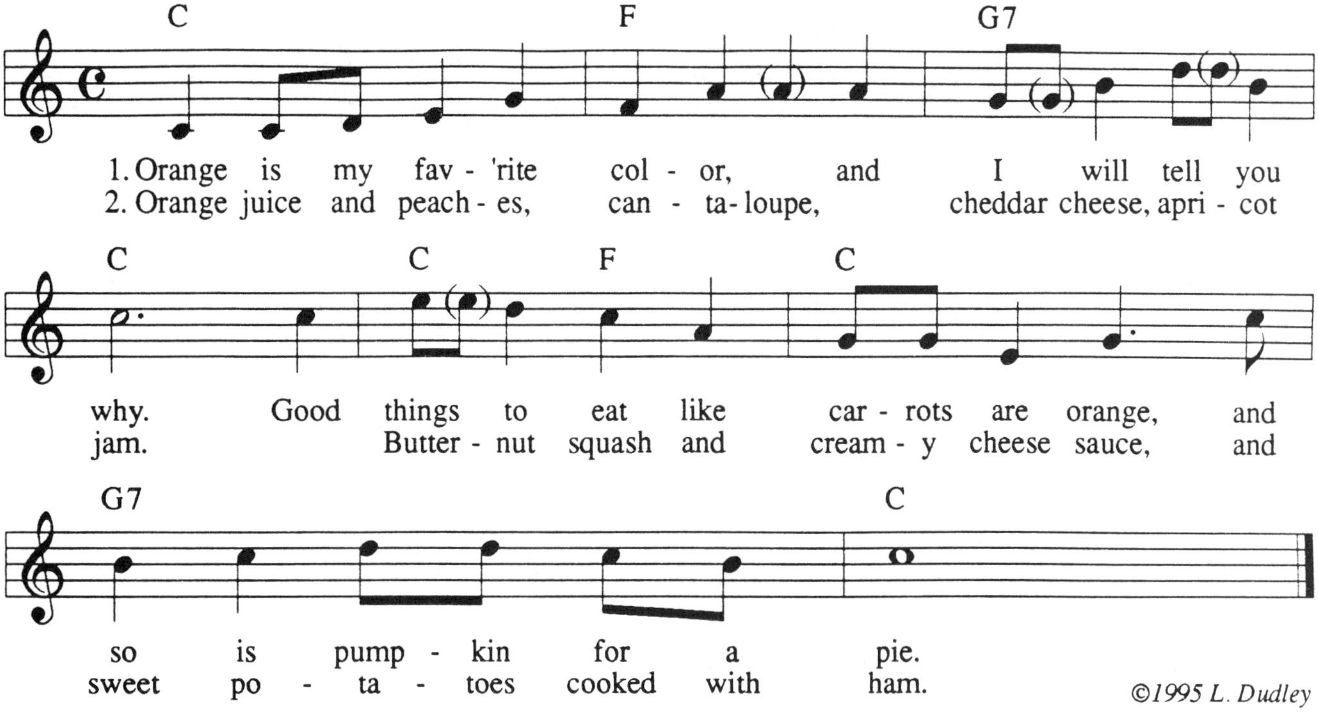
C
F
G7
1. Orange is my fav - 'rite col - or, and I will tell you
2. Orange juice and peach - es, can - ta- loupe, cheddar cheese, apri - cot
C
C
F
C
why. Good things to eat like car - rots are orange, and
jam. Butter - nut squash and cream - y cheese sauce, and
G7
C
so is pump - kin for a pie.
sweet po - ta - toes cooked with ham.

©1995 L. Dudley

ACTIVITY

Color a picture in the frame using only one crayon. This type of picture is known as a monochromatic picture.

Read *The Purple Crayon* by Crockett Johnson or another book about color.

I'm Special

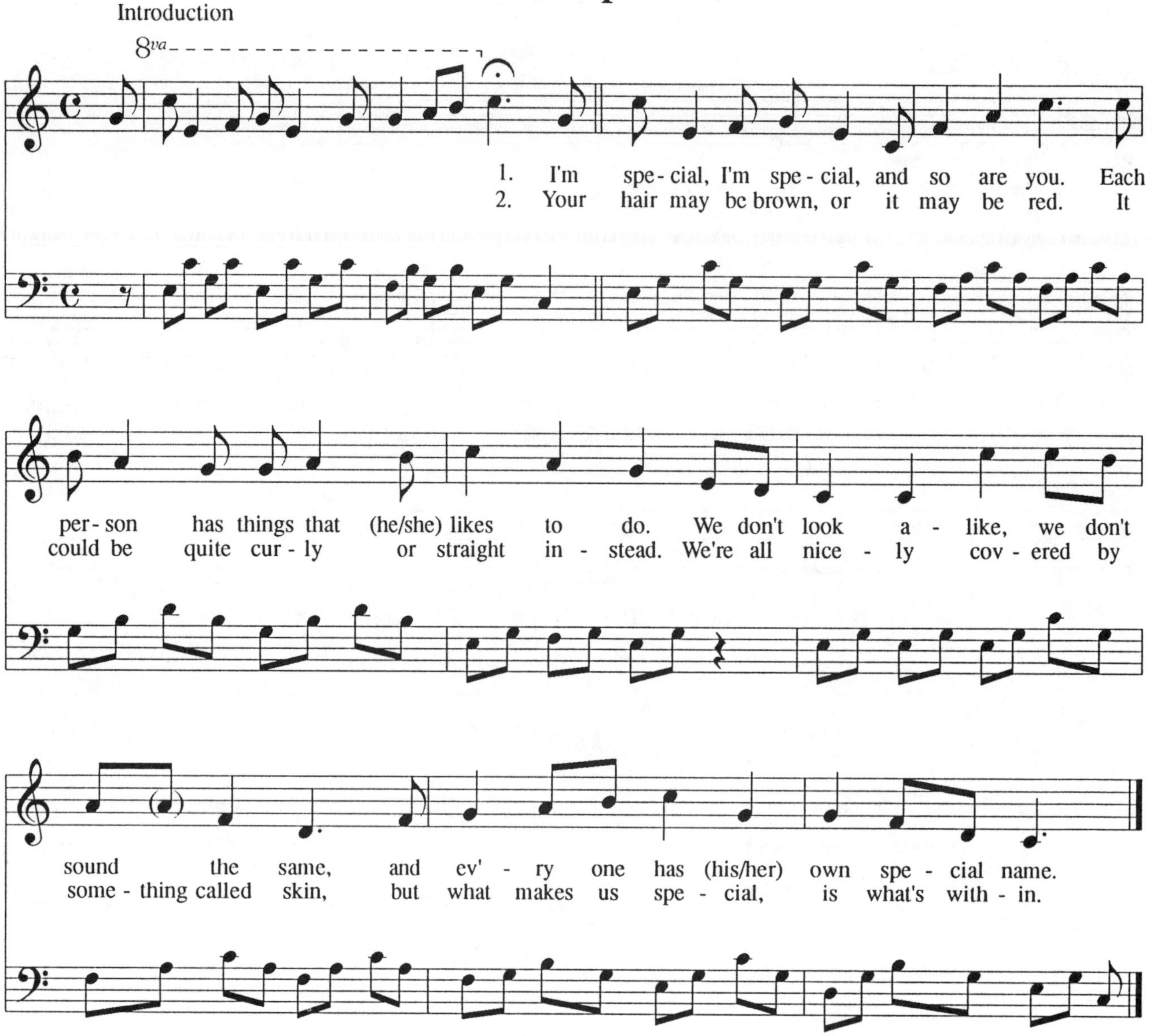
Introduction
8va
1. I'm spe- cial, I'm spe - cial, and so are you. Each
2. Your hair may be brown, or it may be red. It
per- son has things that (he/she) likes to do. We don't look a - like, we don't
could be quite cur - ly or straight in - stead. We're all nice - ly cov - ered by
sound the same, and ev' - ry one has (his/her) own spe - cial name.
some - thing called skin, but what makes us spe - cial, is what's with - in.

© 1995 L. Dudley

I'm Special

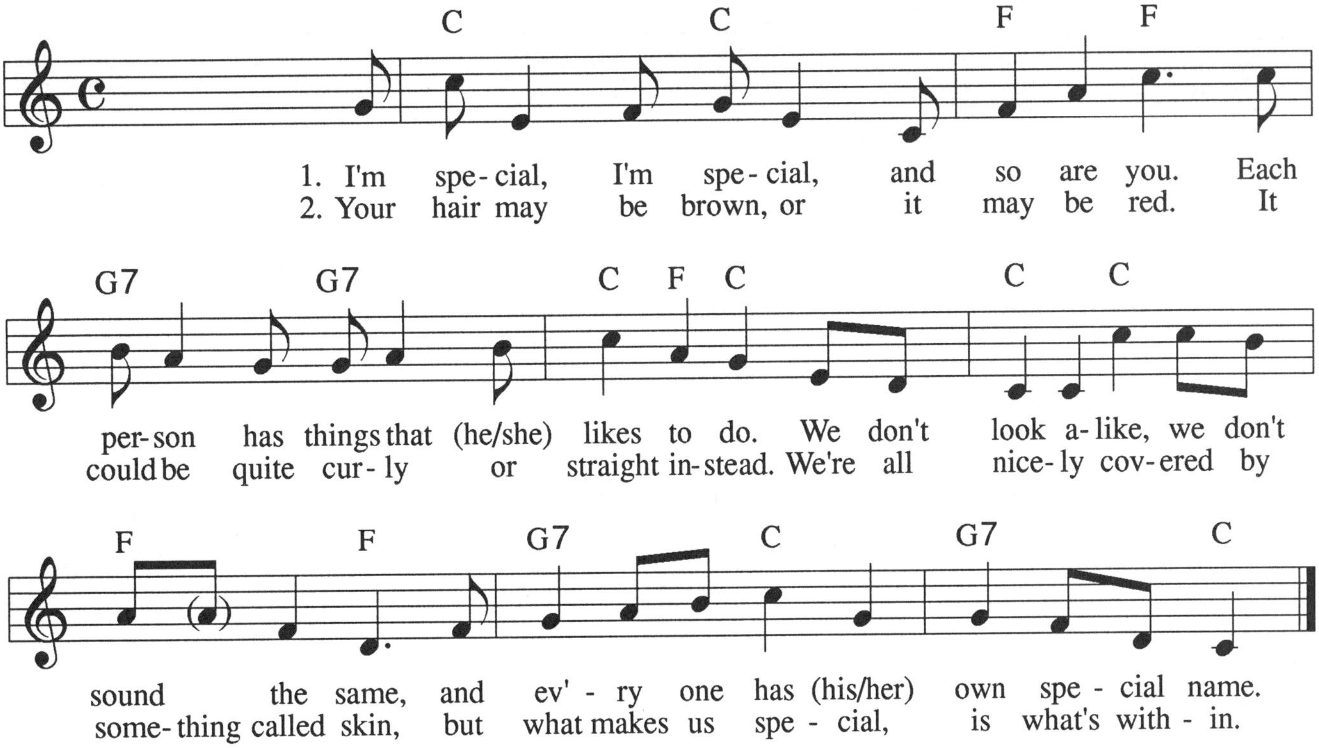

©1995 L. Dudley

ACTIVITY

Write words and phrases on the web to show ways that you are special.

Read *Something Special* by David McPhail or another book about being special.

It's Raining

A bell or triangle may be played on ❉

©1995 L. Dudley

It's Raining

A bell or triangle may be played on ❁

F F C7 F
It's rain - ing, it's rain - ing and I am so hap - py. I'm
I have my um - brel - la, and it is bright red. I'll
C7 G7 C F Dmin
go - ing to dress, and I'll do it so snap - py. I'll put on my
hold it up high to cov - er my head. I'll walk through the
C G7 C F C
boots, my rain coat and hat, then out I will go - the
pud-dles, they'll go split - ter splat - ter. Since I'm wear - ing rain clothes, it
1. G7 C 2. G7 C
rain goes pit pat. real - ly won't mat - ter.

©1995 L. Dudley

ACTIVITY

As a group, make a list of things you can do when it's raining. The list might include watching the rain drops on a window pane. Make a copy of the list for everyone. Keep this list at home so you can do some of the activities when it rains. Draw a check by each activity that you complete.

Read *Listen to the Rain* by Bill Martin Jr. and John Archambault or another book about rain.

The Maple Tree

1. There's a big map - le tree in our front lawn. Its branch-es are
2. On a hot sum - mer day, the tree gives shade. I sit un - der-
emp - ty, the leaves are all gone. Now it is win - ter, our tree is
neath it and drink lem - on - ade. The col - ors of au - tumn are lovely to
1.
rest - ing. Spring will bring leaves, and birds will be nest - ing.
2.
see. There is red, yel - low, orange on our bright ma - ple tree.

The Maple Tree

C F G7 C F
1. There's a big map - le tree in our front lawn. Its branch-es are
2. On a hot sum - mer day, the tree gives shade. I sit un - der-
C D7 G G7 C F
emp - ty, the leaves are all gone. Now it is win - ter, our tree is
neath it and drink lem - on - ade. The col - ors of au - tumn are lovely to
1. C D7 G D7 G
rest - ing. Spring will bring leaves, and birds will be nest - ing.
2. C C C G7 C
see. There is red, yel - low, orange on our bright ma - ple tree.

ACTIVITY

Read about various kinds of trees. Write the names of different kinds of trees on the lines below.

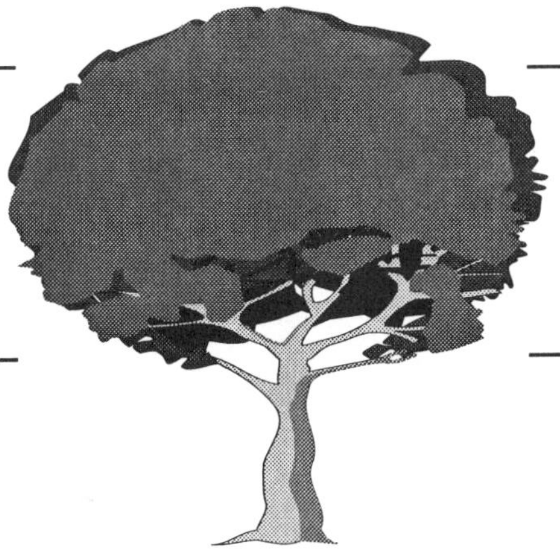

Read *Red Leaf, Yellow Leaf* by Lois Ehlert or another book about trees.

Mothers and Babies

1. A moth- er has a bab - y, and a bab - y has a moth- er. And
some- times their names are diff'- rent from each oth - er. A kit- ten is the bab - y of a
moth - er cat, but a kit- ten can be dang'- rous, if moth- er's a bob - cat.

2. A baby goat is called a kid, a baby pig's a piglet.
A little dog is puppy dear, a little swan's a cygnet.
The baby lions, tigers, and the foxes all are cubs,
but if you are very smart, you won't give them any hugs.

3. A baby deer is called a fawn, a turkey is a poult.
A chicken has some baby chicks, a horse will have a colt.
The mother cow will have a calf, the elephant will too,
and the rhino, hippo, whale, giraffe say calf for babies new.

Mothers and Babies

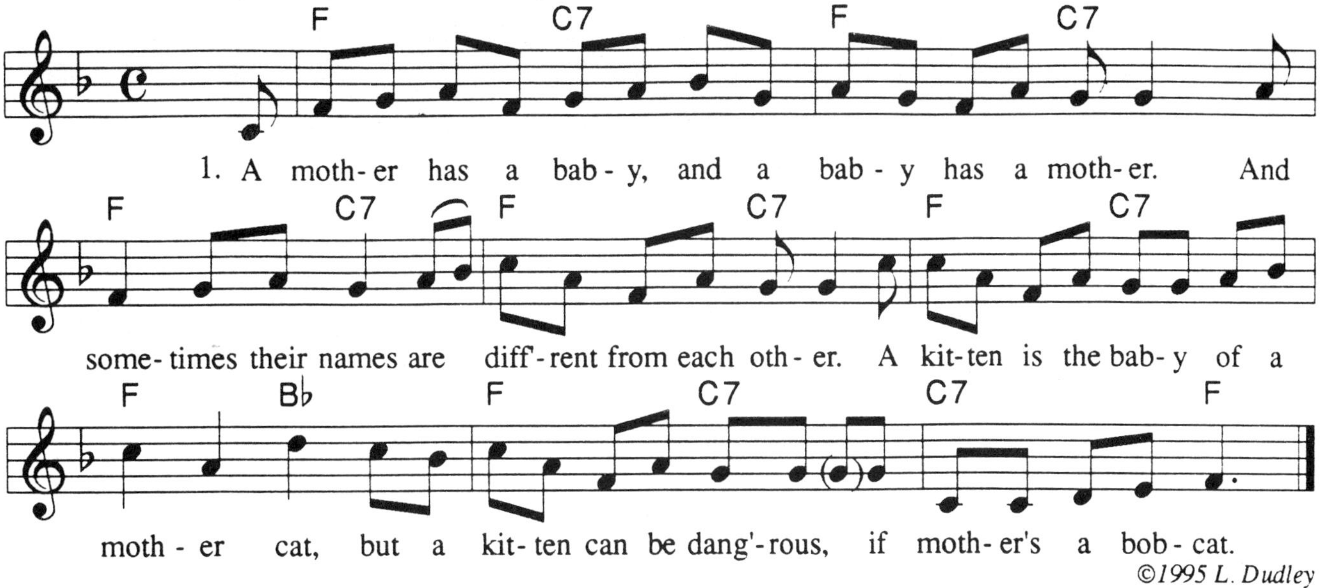
F C7 F C7
1. A moth-er has a bab-y, and a bab-y has a moth-er. And
F C7 F C7 F C7
some-times their names are diff'-rent from each oth-er. A kit-ten is the bab-y of a
F B♭ F C7 C7 F
moth-er cat, but a kit-ten can be dang'-rous, if moth-er's a bob-cat.

©1995 L. Dudley

2. A baby goat is called a kid, a baby pig's a piglet.
A little dog is puppy dear, a little swan's a cygnet.
The baby lions, tigers, and the foxes all are cubs,
but if you are very smart, you won't give them any hugs.

3. A baby deer is called a fawn, a turkey is a poult.
A chicken has some baby chicks, a horse will have a colt.
The mother cow will have a calf, the elephant will too,
and the rhino, hippo, whale, giraffe say calf for babies new.

ACTIVITY

Ask an adult to say the word for a mother animal and then you say the word for the baby animal. Draw a line from the name of the mother to the name of the baby on the lists below.

Read *Why Is Baby Crying?* by Ryerson Johnson or another book about babies.

My Birthday

My birth - day is
spe - cial, 'cause it's just for me; sur - pris - es and pres - ents and
can - dles to see. And some - times my mom says for my spe - cial
treat, we'll have what - ev - er I like to eat.

My Birthday

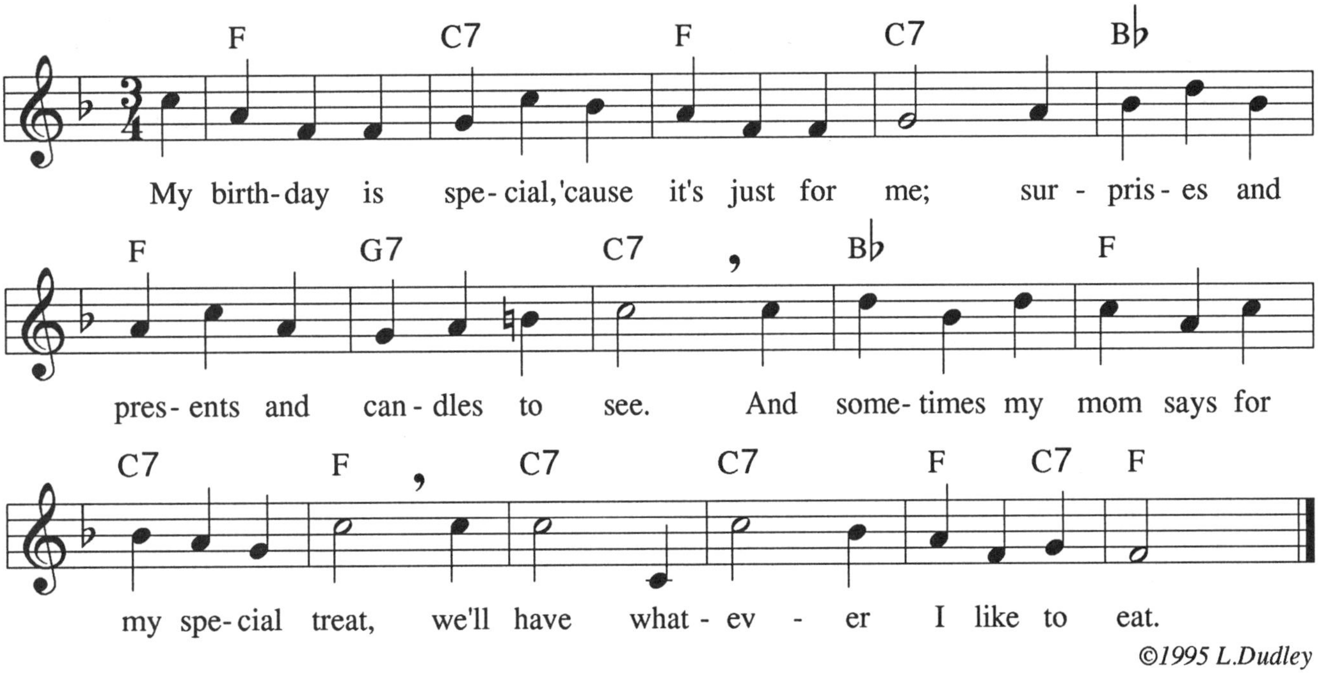

ACTIVITY

Design a cake that you would like to have for your next birthday. Draw the correct number of candles on it.

Read *Birthday Presents* by Cynthia Rylant or another book about birthdays.

My Pen Pal

Introduction
I have a friend in Ger - man-
y, so ver - y far a - way. He'll come to vis - it
me some - day, and this is what I'll say. "Gut - en
(Goot - en
Tag, lieb - er Freund. How are you to - day?" And
Tahk, leeb - er Froint)
Jens will an - swer "Geht's mir gut." Then we'll go out to play.
(Gehts meer goot.)

My Pen Pal

Children may enjoy suggesting another country and putting in a phrase and a child's name from that country. (Example: Ecuador, a Spanish greeting and the name Juan).

ACTIVITY

Write to a pen pal in a different country by yourself or with a group.

Read *Messages in the Mailbox* by Loreen Leedy or another book about pen pals.

The Ocean

Sand blocks may be used on the steady beat.

Gently Rolling

1. I like to go to the o - cean. I'll
2. I like to wade in the wat - er with
take my sho - vel and pail. I'll build a love - ly sand
Dad - dy hold - ing my hand. We'll see some sea - gulls and
cast - le, and watch the boats as they sail.
surf - boards, and hunt for shells in the sand.

© 1995 L. Dudley

The Ocean

Sand blocks may be used on the steady beat.

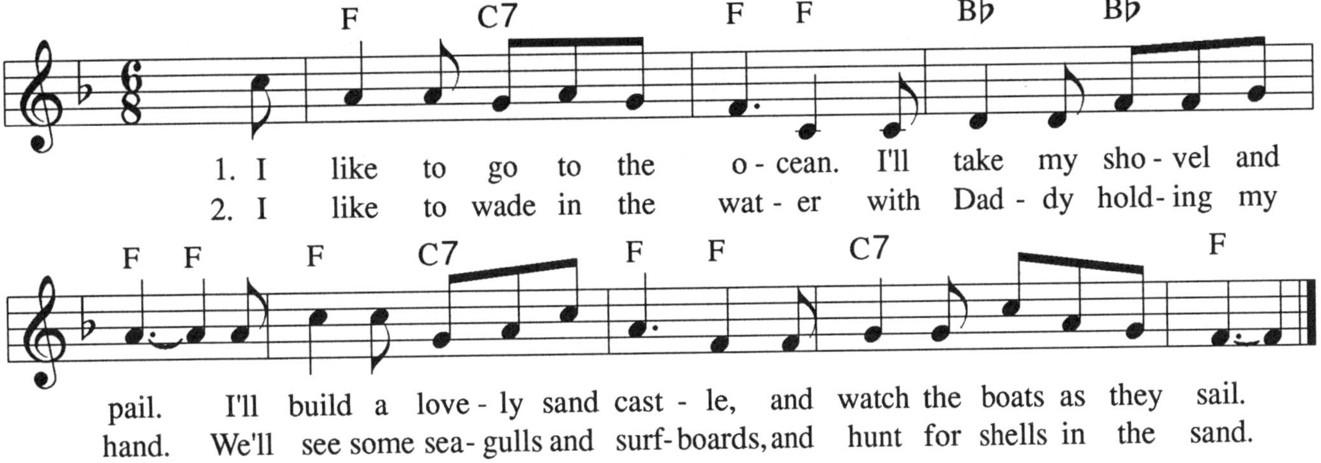
F C7 F F B♭ B♭
1. I like to go to the o - cean. I'll take my sho - vel and
2. I like to wade in the wat - er with Dad - dy hold - ing my
F F F C7 F F C7 F
pail. I'll build a love - ly sand cast - le, and watch the boats as they sail.
hand. We'll see some sea - gulls and surf - boards, and hunt for shells in the sand.

© 1995 L. Dudley

ACTIVITY

Read as much as possible about the ocean. Draw, color, and cut out an animal of the ocean. Glue everyone's animals on a large sheet of paper to make a mural.

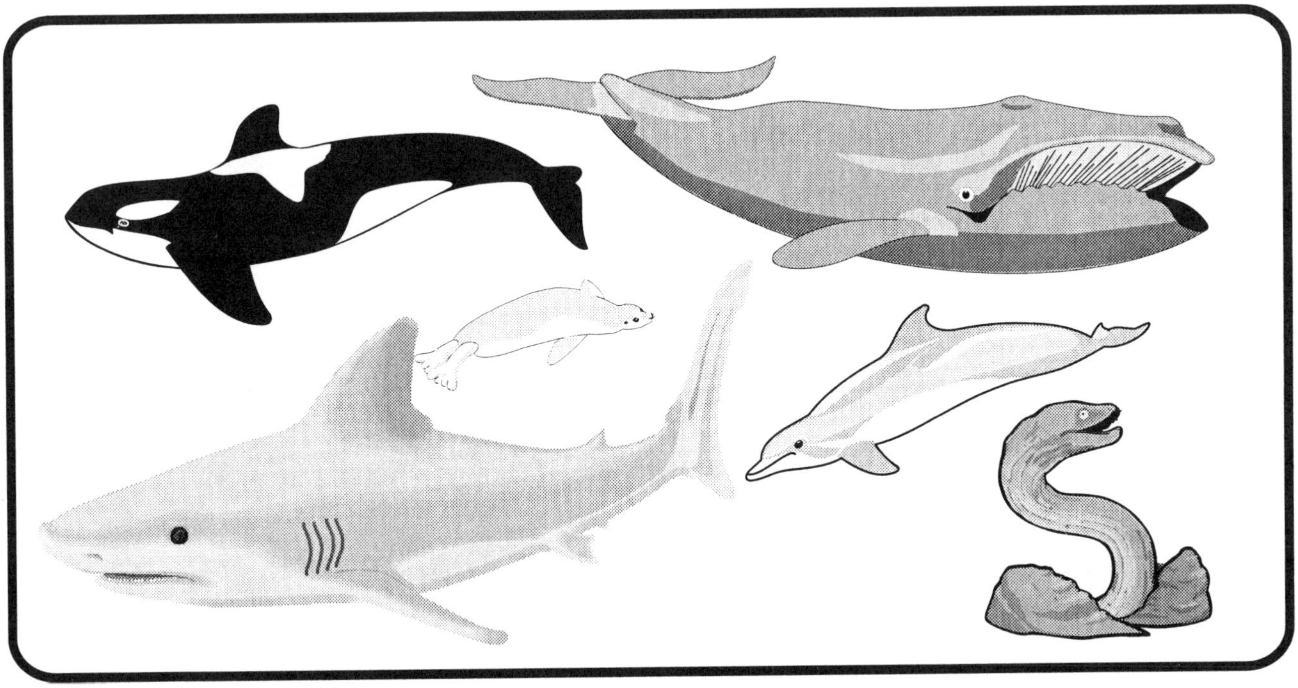

Read *Oceans* by Joy Palmer or another book about oceans.

Opposites

Op - po - sites are not the same. How man - y op - po - sites can you name.
They're as diff' - rent as short and tall. Al - so diff' - rent are big and small.
Fine
Up is the op - po - site of down, and if you smile you don't frown. If you are in you're not out, and when you are cheer - ful you don't pout.
Hap - py's the op - po - site of sad, and good is not the same as bad. Op - po - sites are hot and cold, and a ba - by is young not old.
D.C. al Fine

©1995 L. Dudley

Opposites

F C7 C7 C7 F
Op - po - sites are not the same. How man - y op - po - sites can you name.
F B♭ C7 C7 C7 F
They're as diff - rent as short and tall. Al - so diff - rent are big and small.
Fine
F C7
Up is the op - po - site of down, and
Hap - py's the op - po - site of sad, and
C7 F F
if you smile you don't frown. If you are in you're not
good is not the same as bad. Op - po - sites are hot and
B♭ Gm C7 F D.C. al Fine
out, and when you are cheer - ful you don't pout.
cold, and a ba - by is young not old.

©1995 L. Dudley

ACTIVITY

Ask an adult to say a word that has an opposite meaning. Then say the opposite word. Draw, color, and label opposites in the frame below.

Look at *Exactly the Opposite* by Tana Hoban or another book about opposites.

Our Garden

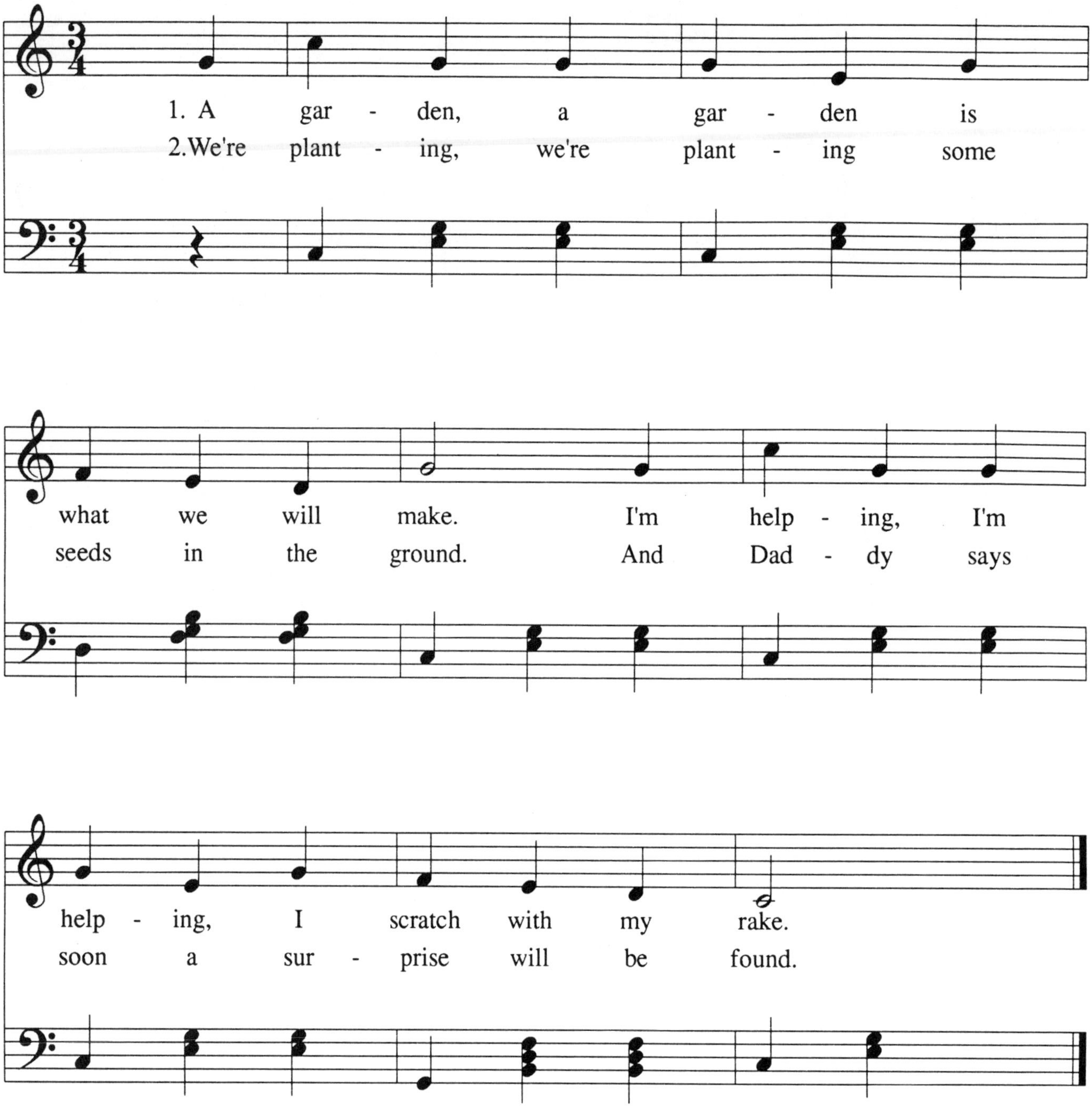
1. A gar - den, a gar - den is
2.We're plant - ing, we're plant - ing some
what we will make. I'm help - ing, I'm
seeds in the ground. And Dad - dy says
help - ing, I scratch with my rake.
soon a sur - prise will be found.

© 1995 L. Dudley

Our Garden

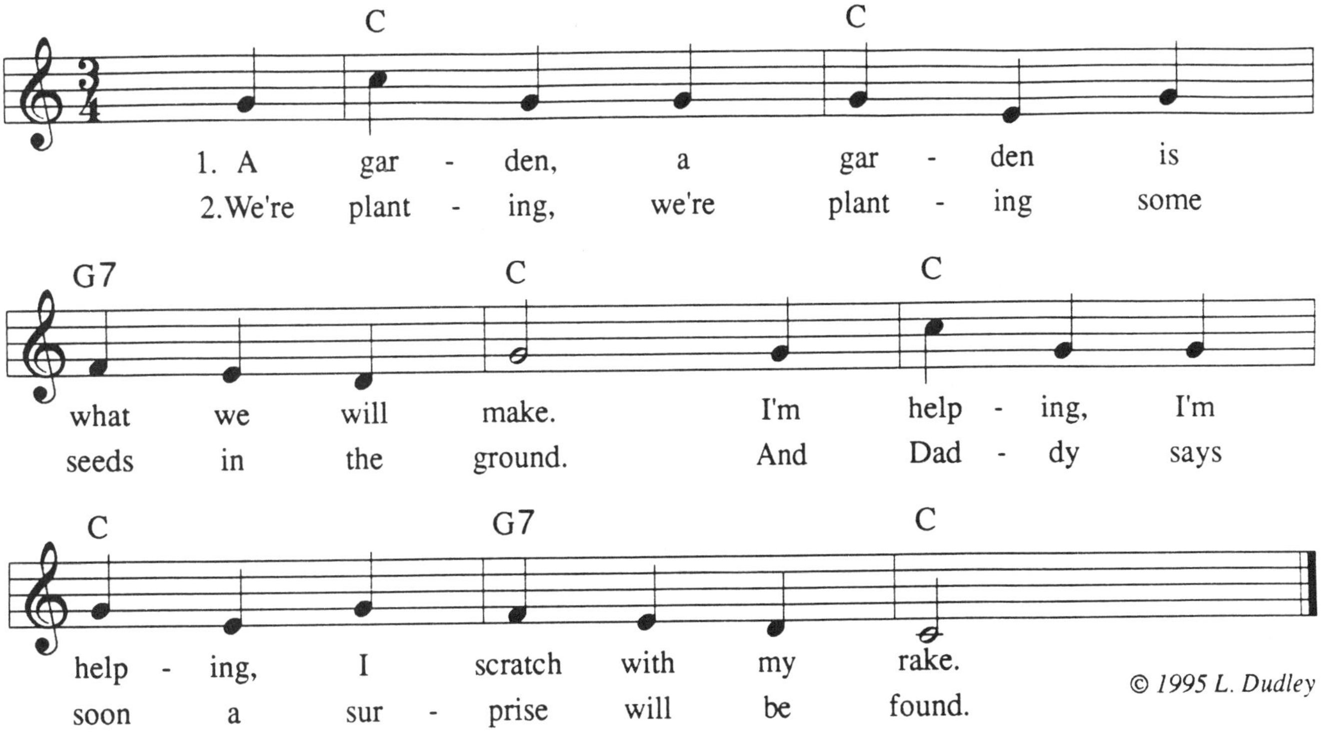
C
C
1. A gar - den, a gar - den is
2.We're plant - ing, we're plant - ing some
G7
C
C
what we will make. I'm help - ing, I'm
seeds in the ground. And Dad - dy says
C
G7
C
help - ing, I scratch with my rake.
soon a sur - prise will be found.

ACTIVITY

Draw the surprise that you think is in the garden. Plant and observe some real plants.

Read *Anna's Garden Songs* by Lena Anderson and Mary Q. Steele or another book about gardens.

A Photographer

A pho - tog - ra- pher takes pic- tures of peo - ple, pla - ces, things. Like
pres- i- dents of the U- nit- ed States and birds with wide- spread wings. A
news - pa - per needs pic - tures of ev' - ry spe- cial e - vent. A pho-
3
tog - ra- pher took my pic - ture for Grand- ma's birth - day pre- sent.

©1995 L. Dudley

A Photographer

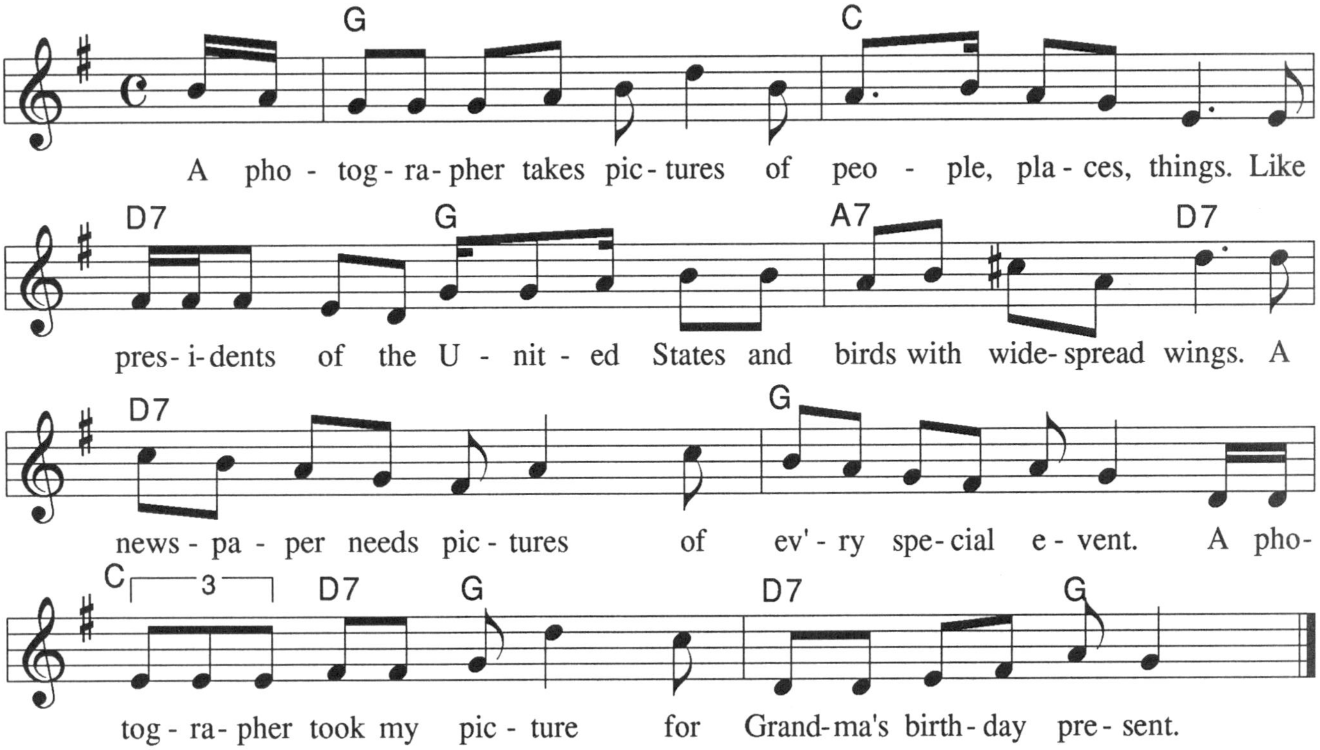
G C
A pho - tog - ra - pher takes pic - tures of peo - ple, pla - ces, things. Like
D7 G A7 D7
pres - i - dents of the U - nit - ed States and birds with wide - spread wings. A
D7 G
news - pa - per needs pic - tures of ev' - ry spe - cial e - vent. A pho -
C 3 D7 G D7 G
tog - ra - pher took my pic - ture for Grand - ma's birth - day pre - sent.

©1995 L. Dudley

ACTIVITY

Read and discuss the work of photographers. Find and cut out photographs from newspapers. Tell or write a story about the photograph such as where, when, and why the photographer took the picture.

Read *Photography* by Tony Freeman or another book about a photographer.

Pumpkins

In our gar - den there's a pump - kin vine, and
it goes here and there. One day when we were pull - ing weeds, we saw
pump - kins ev - 'ry - where. At first they were ti - ny,
like a small green ball. But now they are big and orange and tell us it is Fall.
© 1995 L. Dudley

Pumpkins

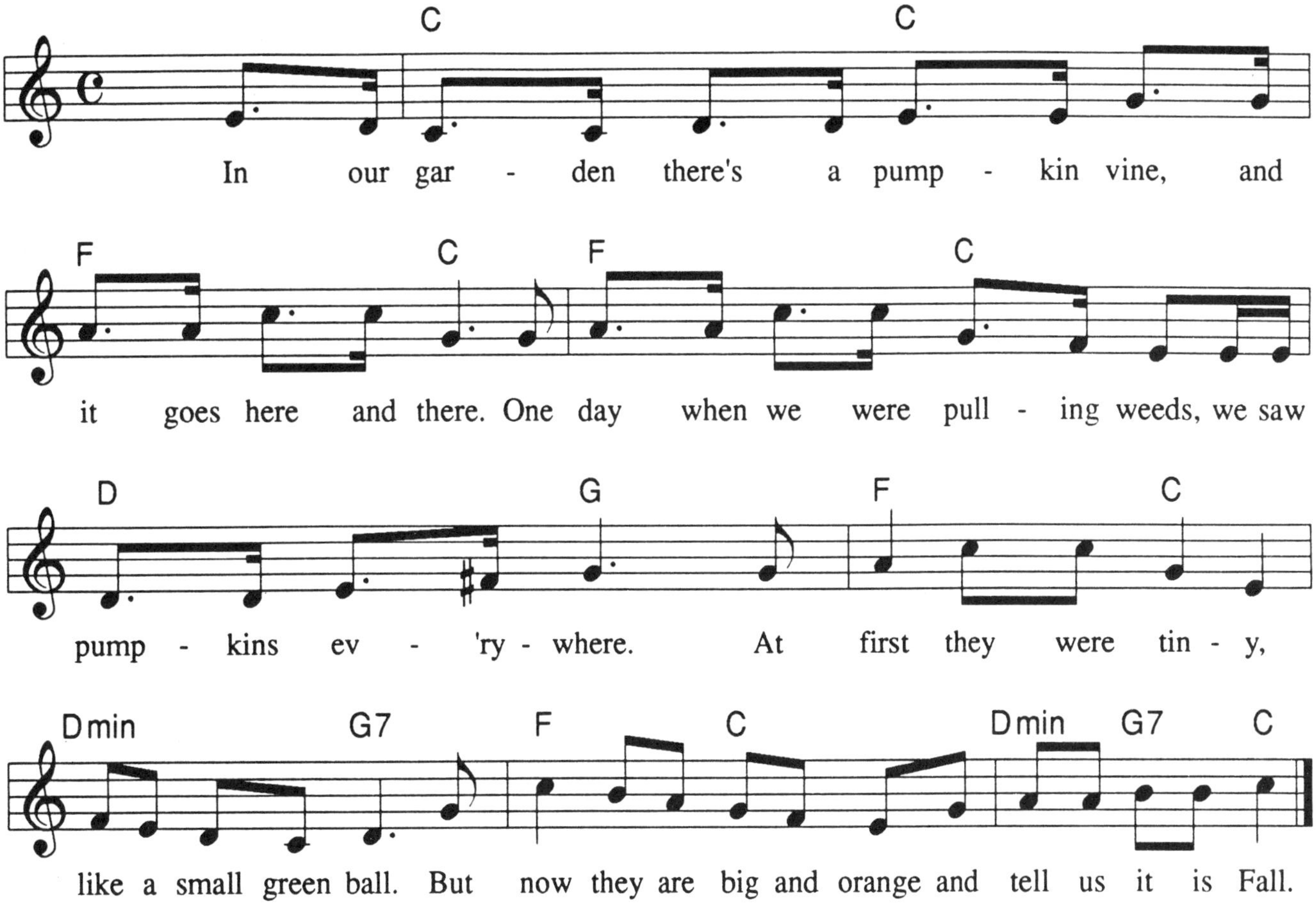

© 1995 L. Dudley

ACTIVITY

Read and discuss how pumpkins are grown. Draw pumpkins on a sheet of white paper. Cut the pumpkins out. Make a pumpkin vine from green paper leaves and green yarn as seen in the illustration below. Glue the vine and pumpkins on heavy paper. These pumpkin vines might be placed on a bulletin board to make a pumpkin patch.

Read *The Pumpkin Patch* by Elizabeth King or another book about pumpkins.

A Rainbow

A wind chime may be played as an introduction.

A rain - bow's some- thing so spe-cial to me. It's peace- ful, love- ly, a
L.H. crosses 8va throughout
pic - ture to see. Soon af- ter a rain if you look up high, there
may be a rain - bow at the edge of the sky. Rain - bow - red, orange and blue,
yel - low, green, vio - let too. A rain - bow ap - pears when the
sun starts to shine, and on - ly re- mains for a ver - y short time.

A Rainbow

A wind chime may be played as an introduction.

©1995 L. Dudley

ACTIVITY

Discuss how a real rainbow is made in the sky. Paint a rainbow on paper using only the primary colors to make secondary colors such as mixing blue and red to get purple.

Read A *Rainbow of My Own* by Don Freeman or another book about a rainbow.

Recycle

1. Re - cy - cle, re - cy - cle, let's look in the trash.
2. Save pa - pers and bot - tles and all your cans too.
Wash out the cans, with your foot go smash, smash. Re - cy- cle, re- cy - cle, don't
Pick up the lit - ter let's make things look new. Put pa- pers in bun- dles, take
throw things a- way. For they can be used in some oth - er way.
off bot - tle tops, and now they can go in the re - cy - cle box.

©1995 L. Dudley

Recycle

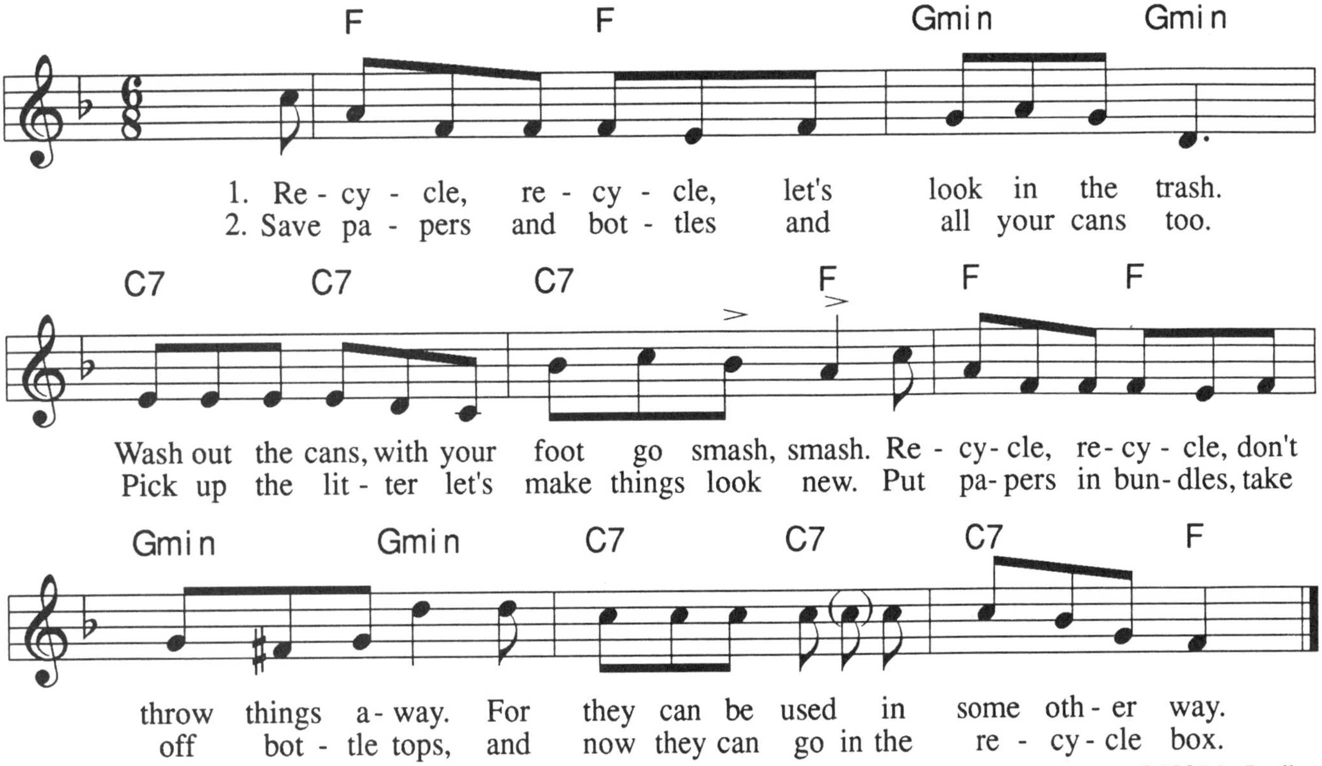
F F Gmin Gmin
1. Re - cy - cle, re - cy - cle, let's look in the trash.
2. Save pa - pers and bot - tles and all your cans too.
C7 C7 C7 F F F
Wash out the cans, with your foot go smash, smash. Re - cy- cle, re- cy - cle, don't
Pick up the lit - ter let's make things look new. Put pa- pers in bun- dles, take
Gmin Gmin C7 C7 C7 F
throw things a- way. For they can be used in some oth - er way.
off bot - tle tops, and now they can go in the re - cy- cle box.

©1995 L. Dudley

ACTIVITY

Draw a design on a large paper grocery bag. Use the bag for storing newspapers you will recycle.

Read *Recycle* by Gail Gibbons or another book about recycling.

The Seasons

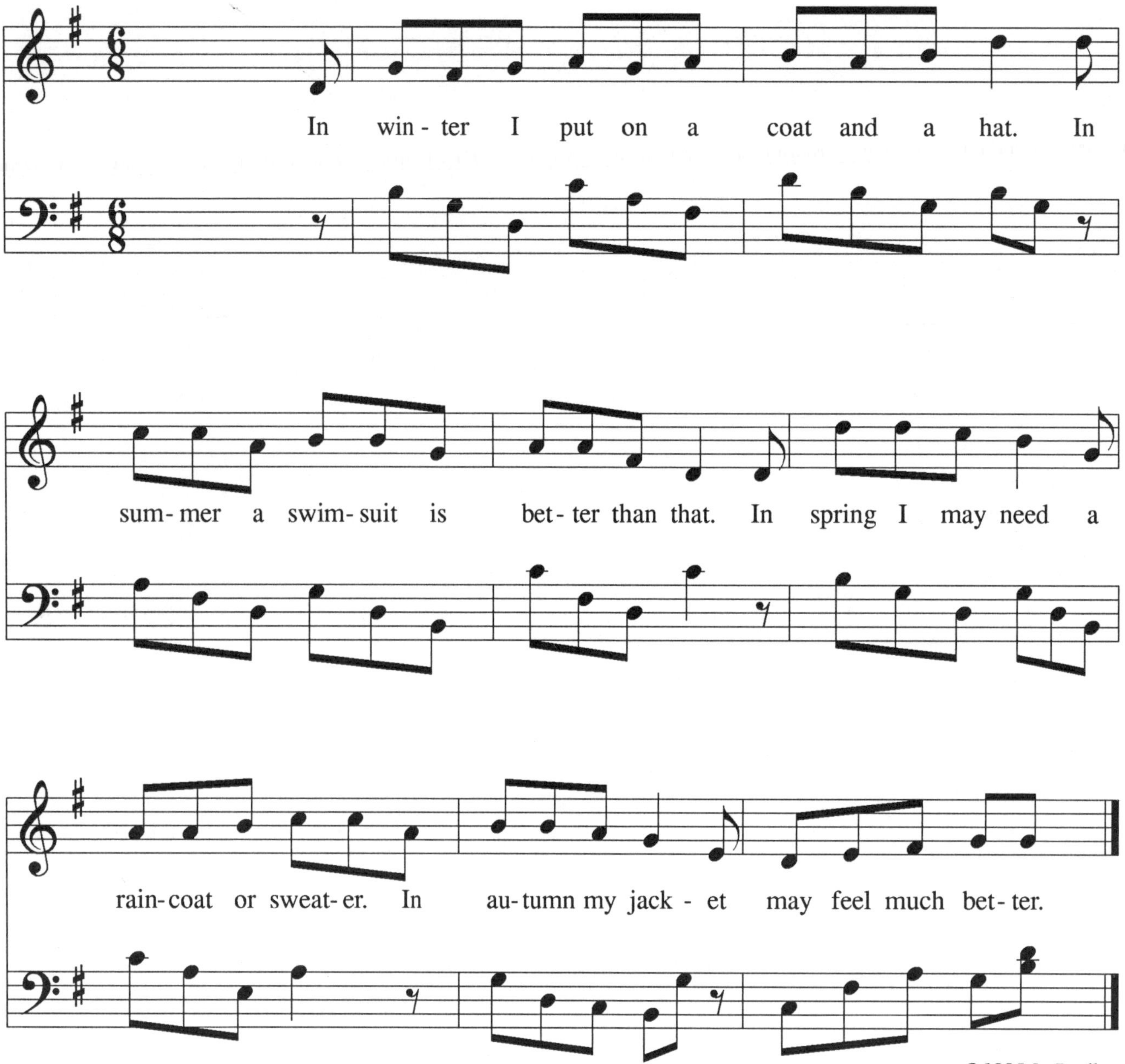

In win - ter I put on a coat and a hat. In
sum- mer a swim- suit is bet- ter than that. In spring I may need a
rain- coat or sweat- er. In au- tumn my jack - et may feel much bet- ter.

©1995 L. Dudley

The Seasons

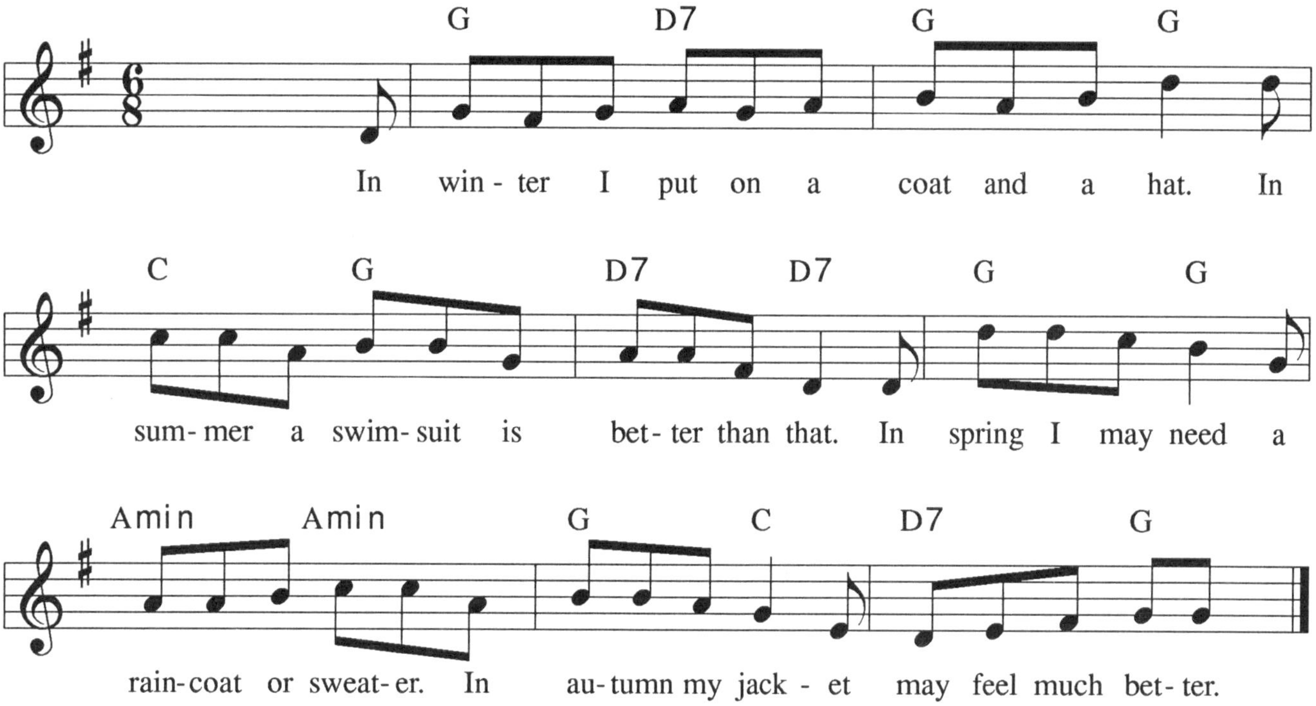
G D7 G G
In win - ter I put on a coat and a hat. In
C G D7 D7 G G
sum- mer a swim- suit is bet- ter than that. In spring I may need a
Amin Amin G C D7 G
rain- coat or sweat- er. In au- tumn my jack - et may feel much bet- ter.

©1995 L. Dudley

ACTIVITY

Draw a picture in each of the sections to show the four seasons where you live. Discuss the seasons in other parts of the world.

WINTER	SPRING
SUMMER	**AUTUMN**

Read *Why Do We Have Different Seasons?* by Isaac Asimov or another book about seasons.

Shapes

1. There are three sides on a tri - an - gle, and three wheels on a trike. A cir - cle's round just like the sun or two wheels on a bike.
2. A square is eith - er big or small, and all sides are the same. But if a cir - cle's kind of long, an el - lipse is its name.
3. There is one more shape that you should know, and here's a lit - tle clue. Two sides are short, two sides are long, it has four cor - ners too.
4. This shape could be a win - dow frame, a cake - pan, a traf - fic light. Now if you said a rec - tan - gle, you real - ly have it right.

©1995 L. Dudley

Shapes

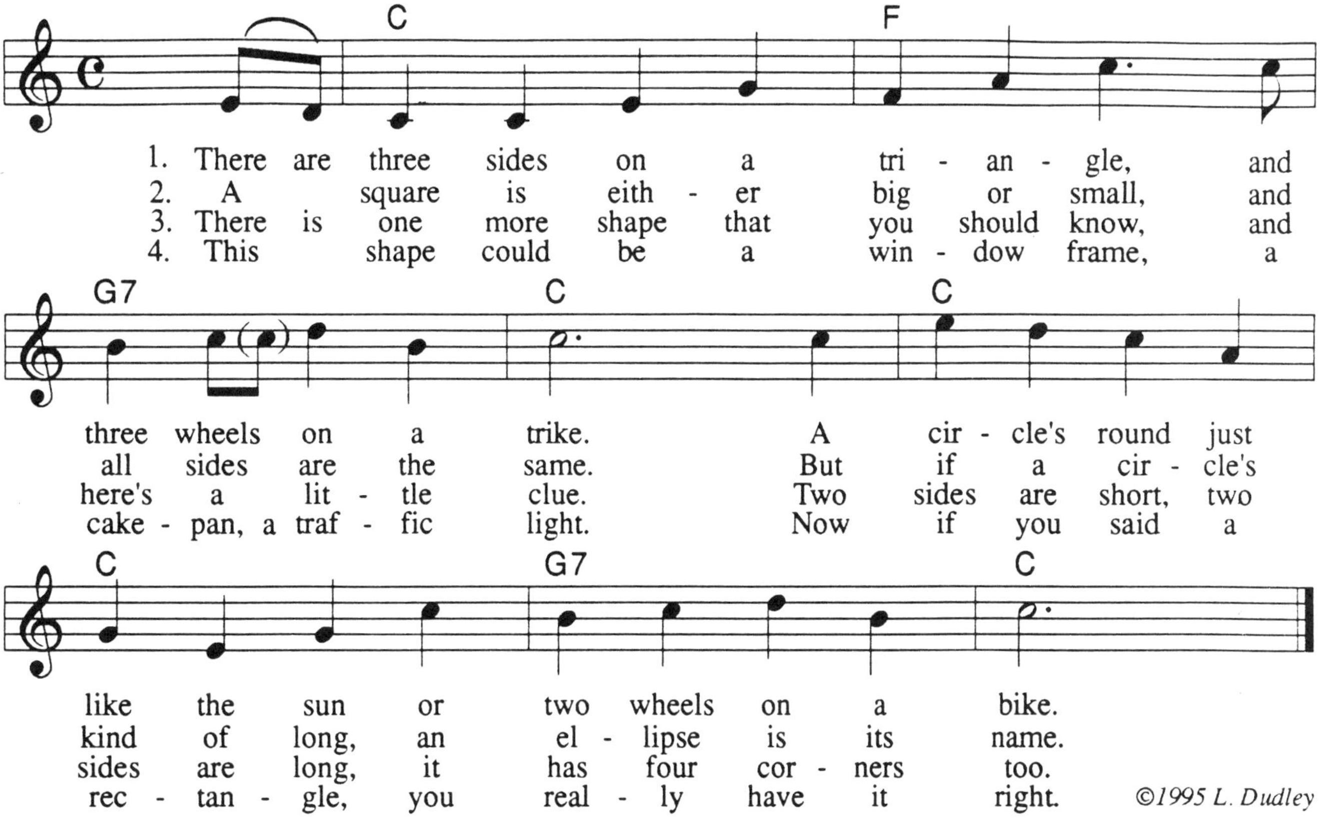
C
F
1. There are three sides on a tri - an - gle, and
2. A square is eith - er big or small, and
3. There is one more shape that you should know, and
4. This shape could be a win - dow frame, a
G7
C
C
three wheels on a trike. A cir - cle's round just
all sides are the same. But if a cir - cle's
here's a lit - tle clue. Two sides are short, two
cake - pan, a traf - fic light. Now if you said a
C
G7
C
like the sun or two wheels on a bike.
kind of long, an el - lipse is its name.
sides are long, it has four cor - ners too.
rec - tan - gle, you real - ly have it right.
©1995 L. Dudley

ACTIVITY

Match the word with each shape. Color only the shapes that are named in the song. Ask an adult to say a riddle about one of the shapes, and you guess the name of the shape in the riddle.

Triangle

Square

Circle

Ellipse

Rectangle

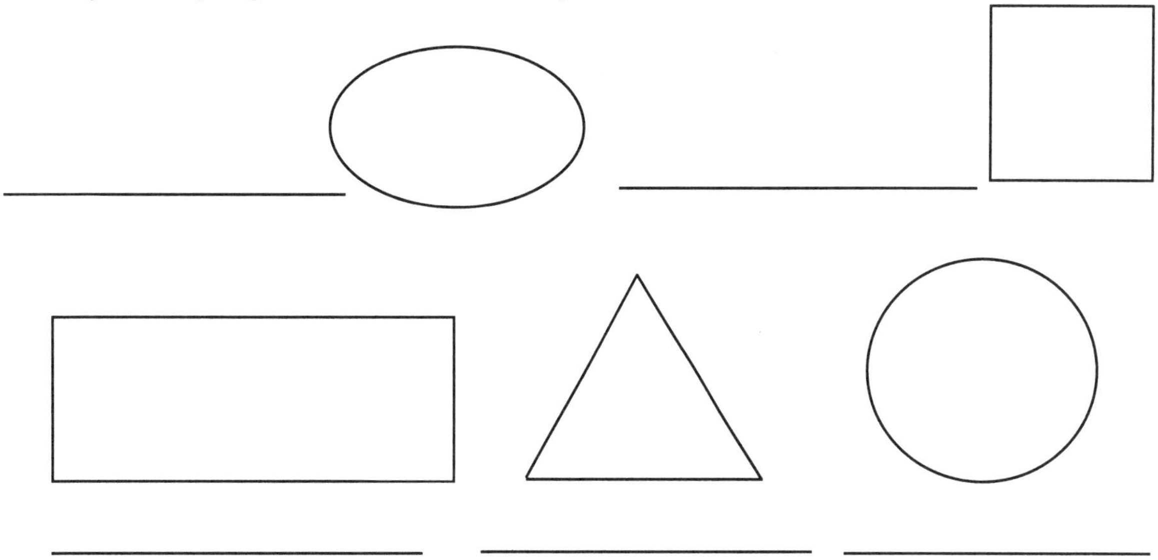

Read *The Shape Game* by Paul Rogers or another book about shapes.

Shoestrings

Shoe- strings can be short, and shoe - strings can be thin. Some are long and wide and
won't stay in. Mine were plain old white, but now they are grey.
Guess I'll take them out and put them a- way. And now it's blue ones and black ones,
orange, yel - low, pink. Red ones with pur - ple and green spots, I think.
Pic- tures of space- men and tur - tles too, and may - be an - i - mals from the zoo.

©1995 L. Dudley

Shoestrings

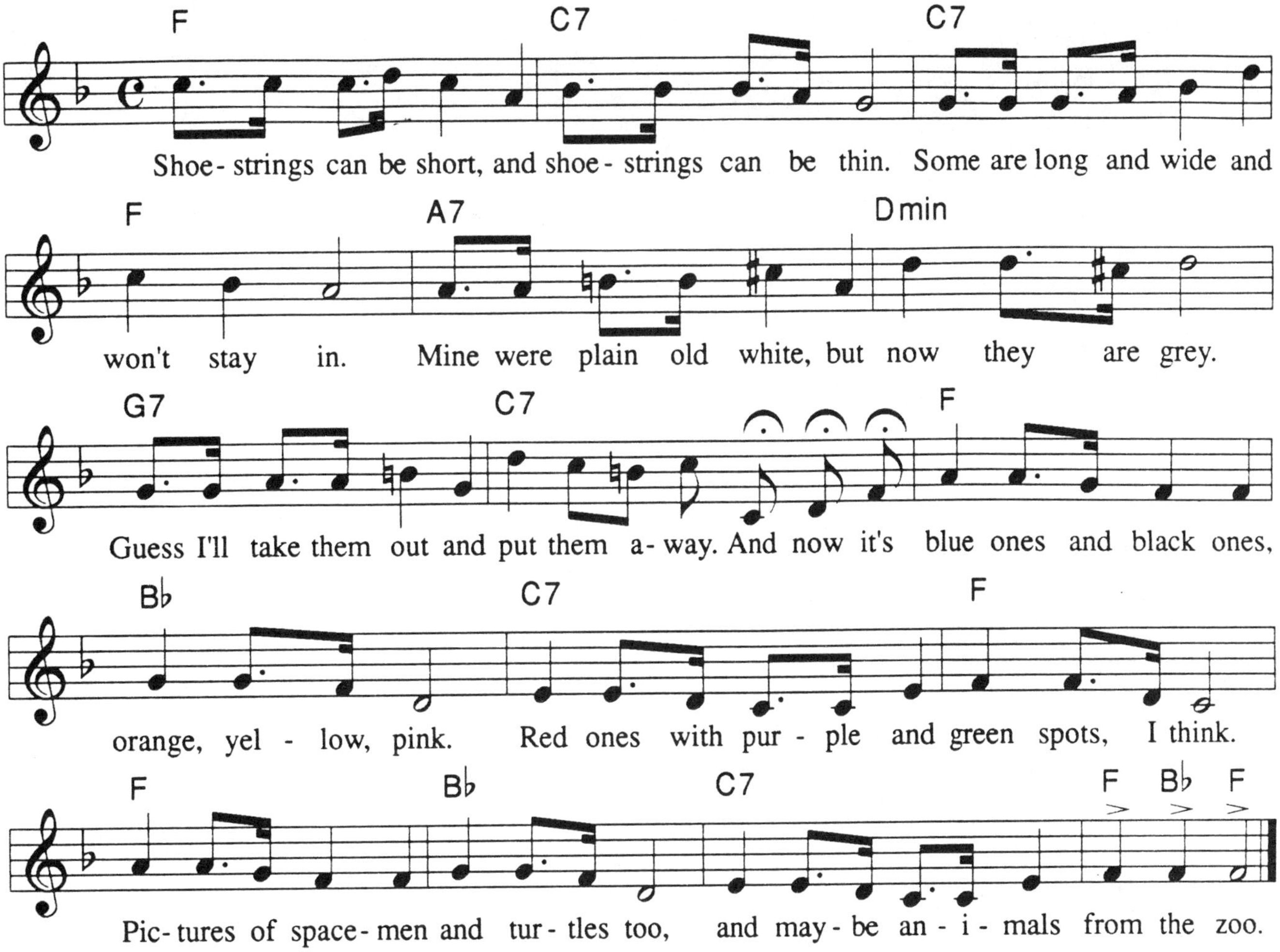
F C7 C7
Shoe- strings can be short, and shoe- strings can be thin. Some are long and wide and
F A7 Dmin
won't stay in. Mine were plain old white, but now they are grey.
G7 C7 F
Guess I'll take them out and put them a- way. And now it's blue ones and black ones,
B♭ C7 F
orange, yel - low, pink. Red ones with pur - ple and green spots, I think.
F B♭ C7 F B♭ F
Pic- tures of space- men and tur- tles too, and may- be an - i - mals from the zoo.

©1995 L. Dudley

ACTIVITY

Measure and record the length of each of the shoestrings. Color designs on the shoestrings for shoes that you would like to wear. Measure real shoestrings.

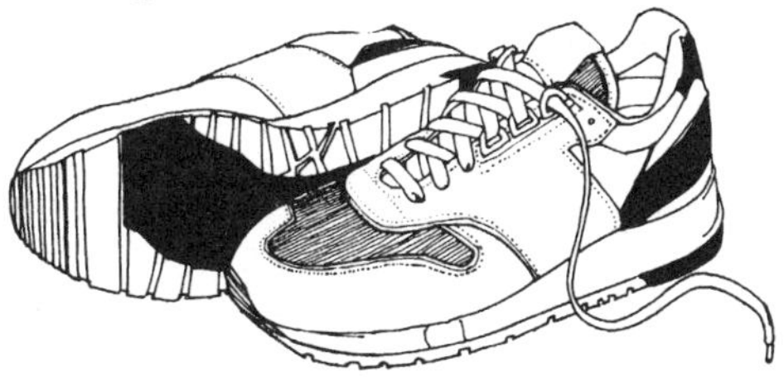

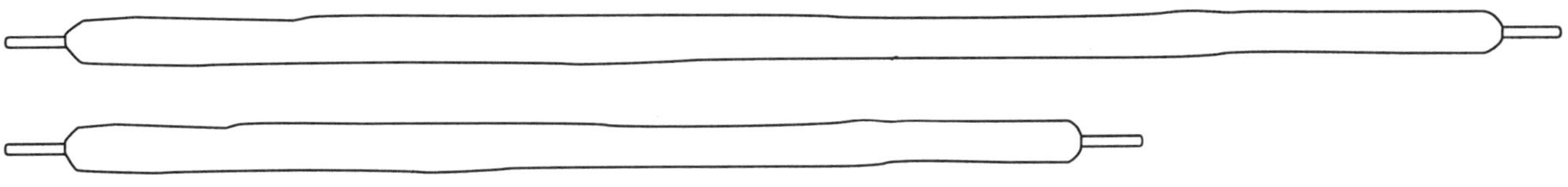

Read *Shoes* by Elizabeth Winthrop or another book about shoes.

Things I Like

1. I like lol - li - pops and lem - on drops, jump - ing rope and fish - ing,
2. I like ice cream cones and chick - en bones, swim - ming in the pool,
3. I like milk to drink and cook - ies pink, help - ing Mom make cake,
4. I like shish - ka - bob and corn on the cob, pic - nics in the park,
5. I like straw - ber - ries and sour cher - ries, go - ing to the zoo,
dig - ging worms and read - ing books, and goo - ey mud for squish - ing.
build - ing blocks and run - ning fast, and learn - ing things at school.
shov' - ling snow and snow - ball fights, and swim - ming in the lake.
fly - ing kites and watch - ing clouds, and fire - flies in the dark.
va - ca - tions and rol - ler skates, and my new ten - nis shoes.

©1995 L. Dudley

Things I Like

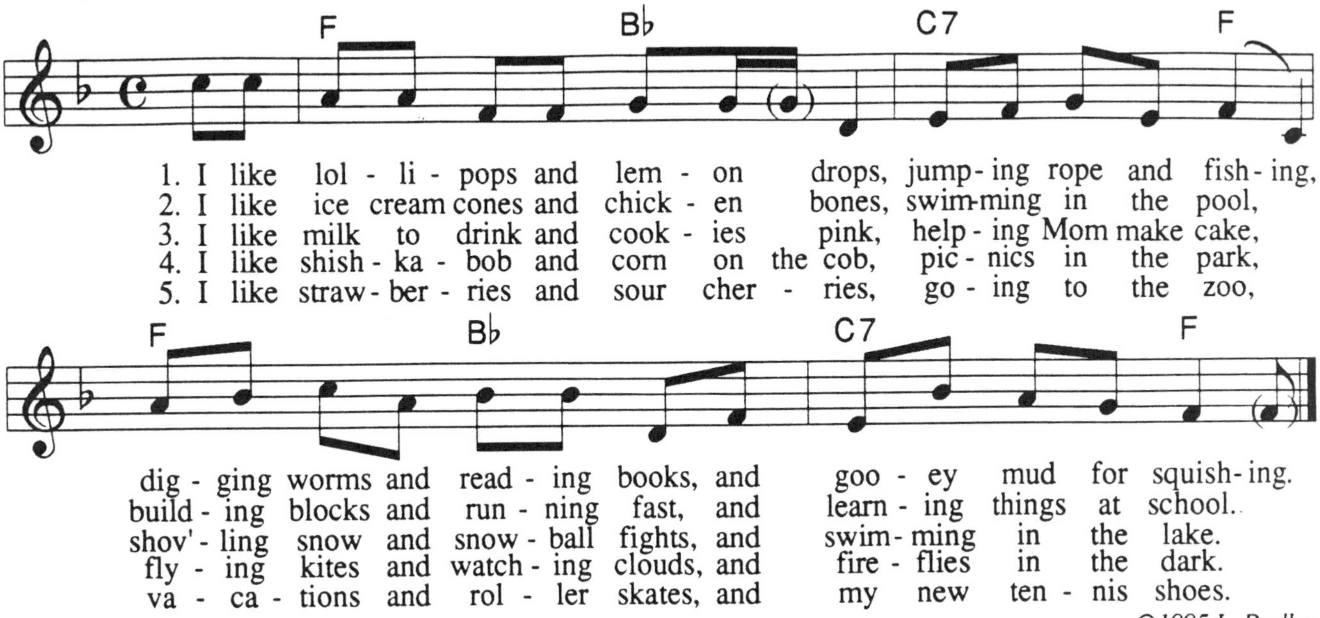

©1995 L. Dudley

ACTIVITY

Write and illustrate a booklet of things you like. It might be an alphabet book.

Read *I Like Books* by Anthony Browne or another book about things people like.

Time

Rhythm instruments may be used for the tick-tock effect of the clock.

Introduction
Lunch time, nap time, a pro- gram on T. V.
Bath time, stor- y time, bed time for me. We all need some- thing that
goes tick tock. What do we need? It's called a clock.

© 1995 L. Dudley

Time

Rhythm instruments may be used for the tick-tock effect of the clock.

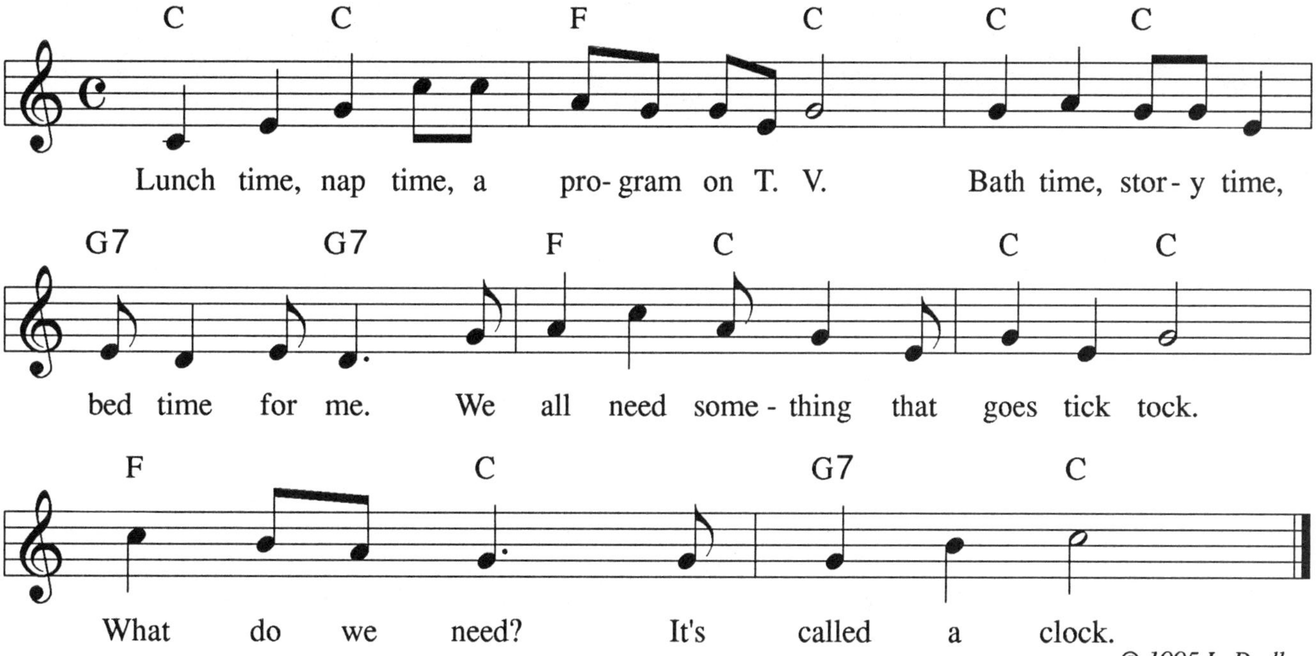
C C F C C C
Lunch time, nap time, a pro- gram on T. V. Bath time, stor - y time,
G7 G7 F C C C
bed time for me. We all need some - thing that goes tick tock.
F C G7 C
What do we need? It's called a clock.

© 1995 L. Dudley

ACTIVITY

Draw the minute hands and the hour hands on the clocks to show different times of the day.

Read *Around the Clock with Harriet* by Betsy and Giulio Maestro or another book about clocks or time.

Toy Train

A whistle or kazoo may be blown at the ❈

©1995 L. Dudley

Toy Train

A whistle or kazoo may be blown at the ❊

F
B♭
I push the but - ton, and what do you sup - pose? A -
en - gine, coal car, and may - be a ca - boose.
C7
1. F
2. F
round the track my toy train goes. An spe - cial use. And it's
Each one has a
F
B♭
C7
chug-a-chug-a, chug-a-chug-a, and we're off at last. Chug-a-chug-a, chug-a-chug, the
F
F
B♭
whist-le gives a blast. Chug-a-chug-a, chug-a-chug-a com - ing round the bend.
C7
C7
F
B♭
F
Toot, toot, the ride will end.

©1995 L. Dudley

ACTIVITY

Make a 'Book Record Train' using 4" x 6" index cards. First make a train engine from paper like the one in the illustration below. Read a book. On an index card draw a train car and write the title of the book on one side and a comment about the book on the opposite side. Store your train cards in a manila envelope. The cars can be lined up behind the engine to make a train.

Read *The Little Engine That Could* by Watty Piper or another book about a toy train.

The Turtle

1. I wish I were a tur - tle, I'd
2. I'd nev - er have to hur - ry. For
live way down low. My house would be right
lunch some bugs I'd snap. I'd pull my head in -
on my back, where ev - er I would go.
side my shell, and then I'd take a nap.

The Turtle

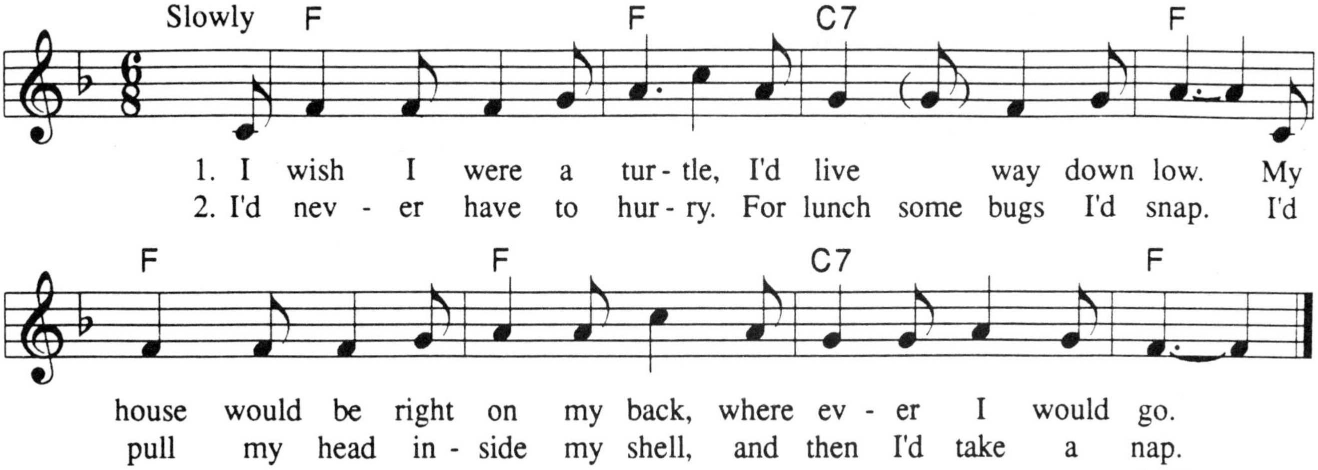
Slowly
F
F
C7
F
1. I wish I were a tur - tle, I'd live way down low. My
2. I'd nev - er have to hur - ry. For lunch some bugs I'd snap. I'd
F
F
C7
F
house would be right on my back, where ev - er I would go.
pull my head in - side my shell, and then I'd take a nap.

ACTIVITY

Read about and discuss turtles, including the size and number of eggs they lay. From clay, make sets of 100-150 turtle eggs. Count the turtle eggs by 1's and by 10's.

Read *The Turtle* by Yvette Metal or another book about a turtle.

Veg'table Soup

©1995 L. Dudley

Veg'table Soup

F C7 F C7
1. It's cold and it's snow - ing, the north wind is blow - ing, so
2. You add on - ions and cab - bage and pep - pers and green beans and
F C7 F F C7
Moth - er got out the crock pot. "My dears don't you know what we
car - rots and ripe red to - ma - toes. Cel - er - y, sweet corn and
F C7 F C7 F
need in this snow is to cook up some soup that is hot. With
pars - ley and green peas and two cups of fine diced po - ta - toes.
F F C7 C7 C7 C7 F F
veg' ta-bles,veg' ta- bles, then add some meat. Veg' ta- bles,veg' ta-bles, can't wait to eat.
F F B♭ B♭ C7 C7 C7 F
Plen-ty of wat- er, some pep- per and spice. Stir it a-round. Oh, my, it smells nice."

©1995 L. Dudley

ACTIVITY

Volunteers bring vegetables to make soup. After the soup is cooked, everyone can eat it. Observe and discuss how the cooked vegetables in the soup changed in color, texture, and taste from the raw vegetables.

Read *Growing Vegetable Soup* by Lois Ehlert or another book about vegetable soup.

Veterinarian

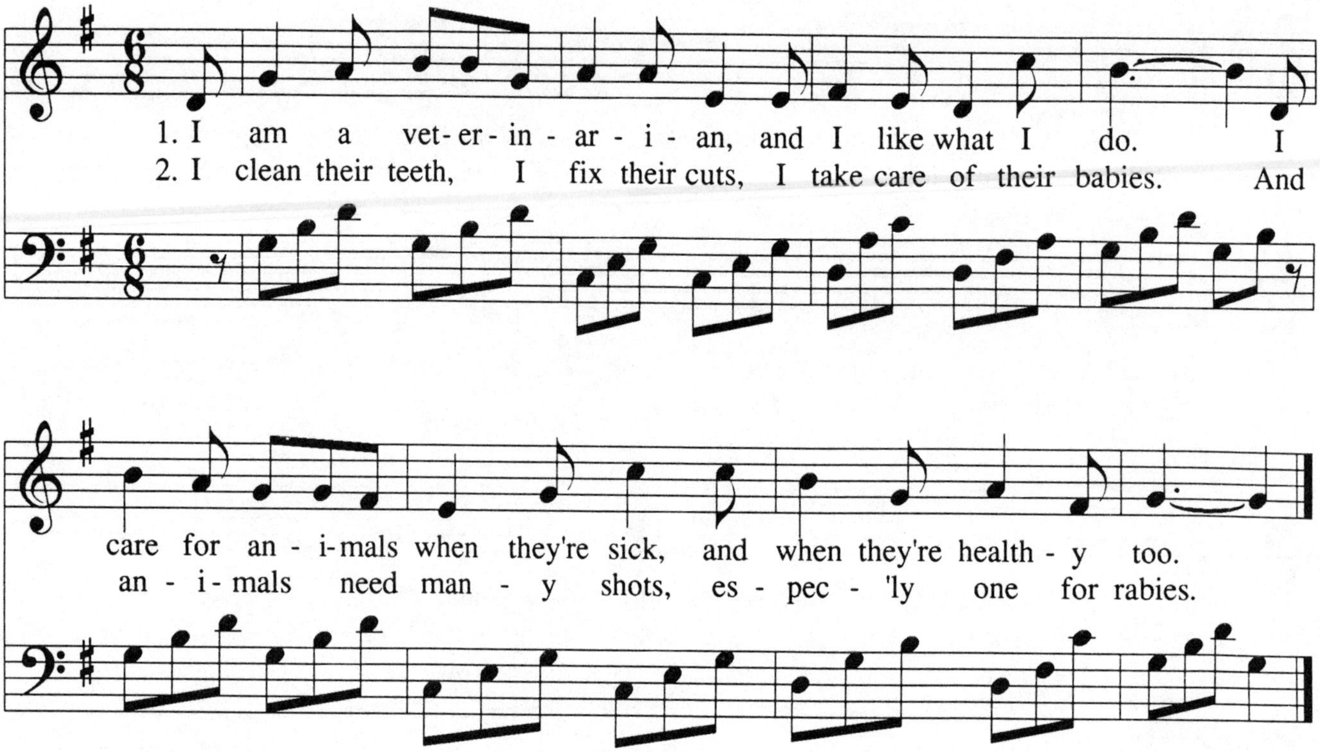
1. I am a vet-er-in-ar-i-an, and I like what I do. I
2. I clean their teeth, I fix their cuts, I take care of their babies. And
care for an-i-mals when they're sick, and when they're health-y too.
an-i-mals need man-y shots, es-pec-'ly one for rabies.

©1995 L. Dudley

Veterinarian

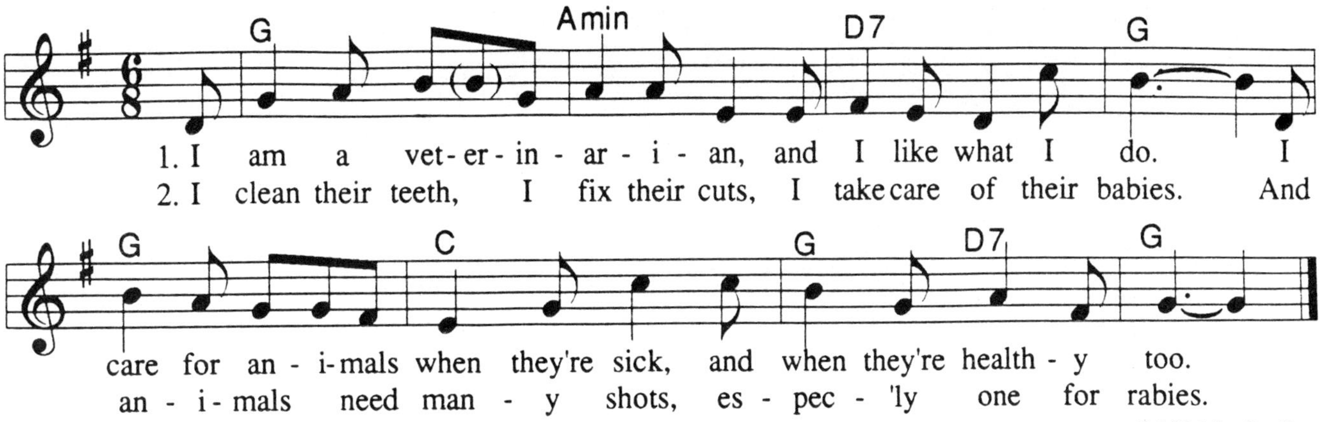
G Amin D7 G
1. I am a vet-er-in-ar-i-an, and I like what I do. I
2. I clean their teeth, I fix their cuts, I take care of their babies. And
G C G D7 G
care for an-i-mals when they're sick, and when they're health-y too.
an-i-mals need man-y shots, es-pec-'ly one for rabies.

©1995 L. Dudley

ACTIVITY

Read about veterinarians. Write a list of things that veterinarians do to care for animals.

___

___

___

___

___

___

___

___

___

___

___

___

___

Read *Taking My Dog to the Vet* by Susan Kuklin or another book about a veterinarian.

Water

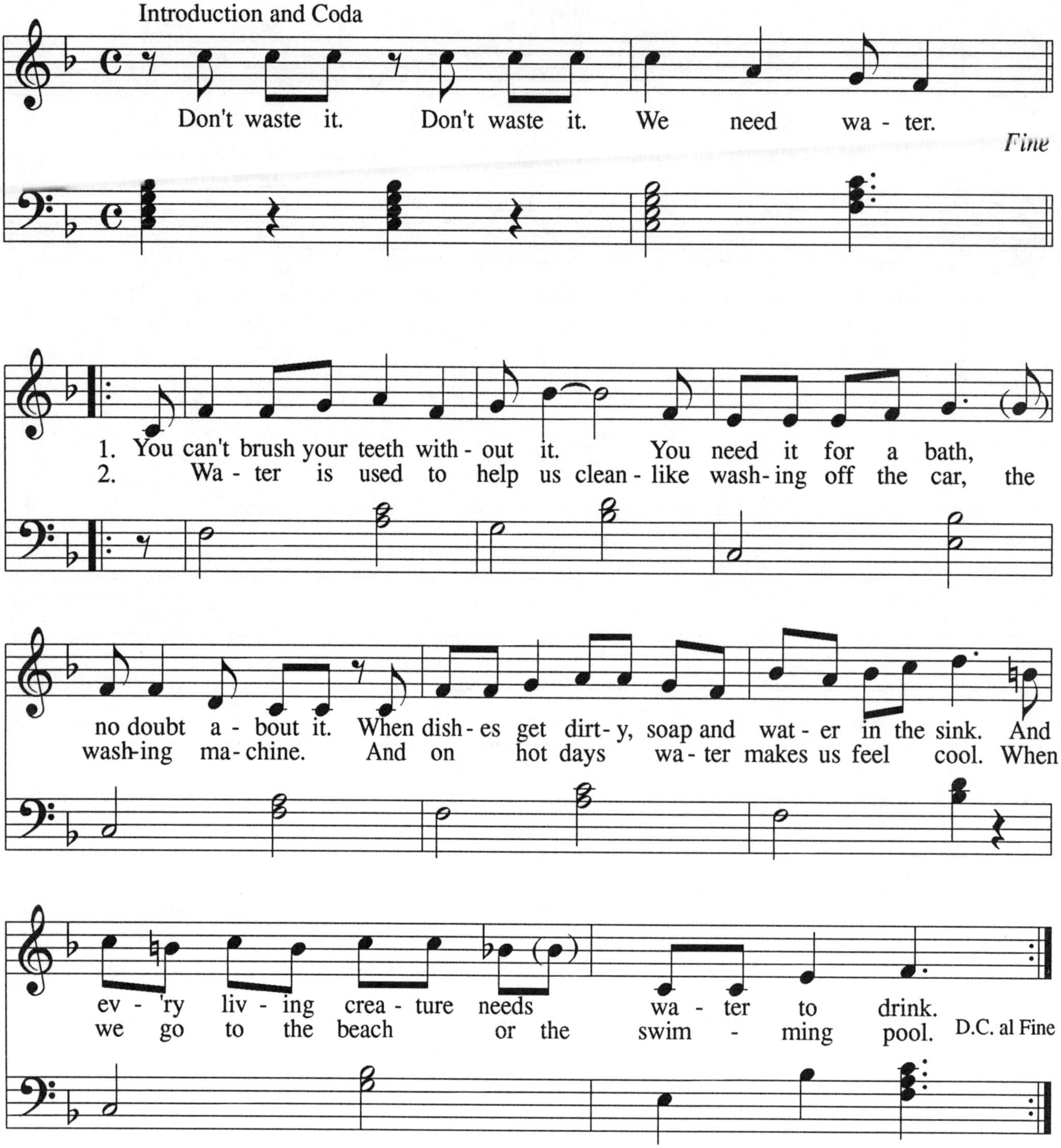

©1995 L. Dudley

Water

Introduction and Coda
C7 C7 C7 C7 F
Don't waste it. Don't waste it. We need wa - ter.
F Gmin C7
1. You can't brush your teeth with - out it. You need it for a bath,
2. Wa - ter is used to help us clean - like wash-ing off the car, the
F F B♭
no doubt a - bout it. When dish - es get dirt - y, soap and wat - er in the sink. And
wash-ing ma - chine. And on hot days wa - ter makes us feel cool. When
C7 C7 F
ev - 'ry liv - ing crea - ture needs wa - ter to drink.
we go to the beach or the swim - ming pool.
To Coda after verse 2

©1995 L. Dudley

ACTIVITY

Discuss ways that we use water. Discuss ways that we can save water. Design a goal card such as the one below and write a goal to show how you will save water.

MY GOAL

I will save water by ______________________________

____

____

Read *Wonderful Water* by Bobbie Kalman & Janine Schaub or another book about water.

A Week

©1995 L. Dudley

❊ Pat knees once, clap hands twice throughout refrain.

A Week

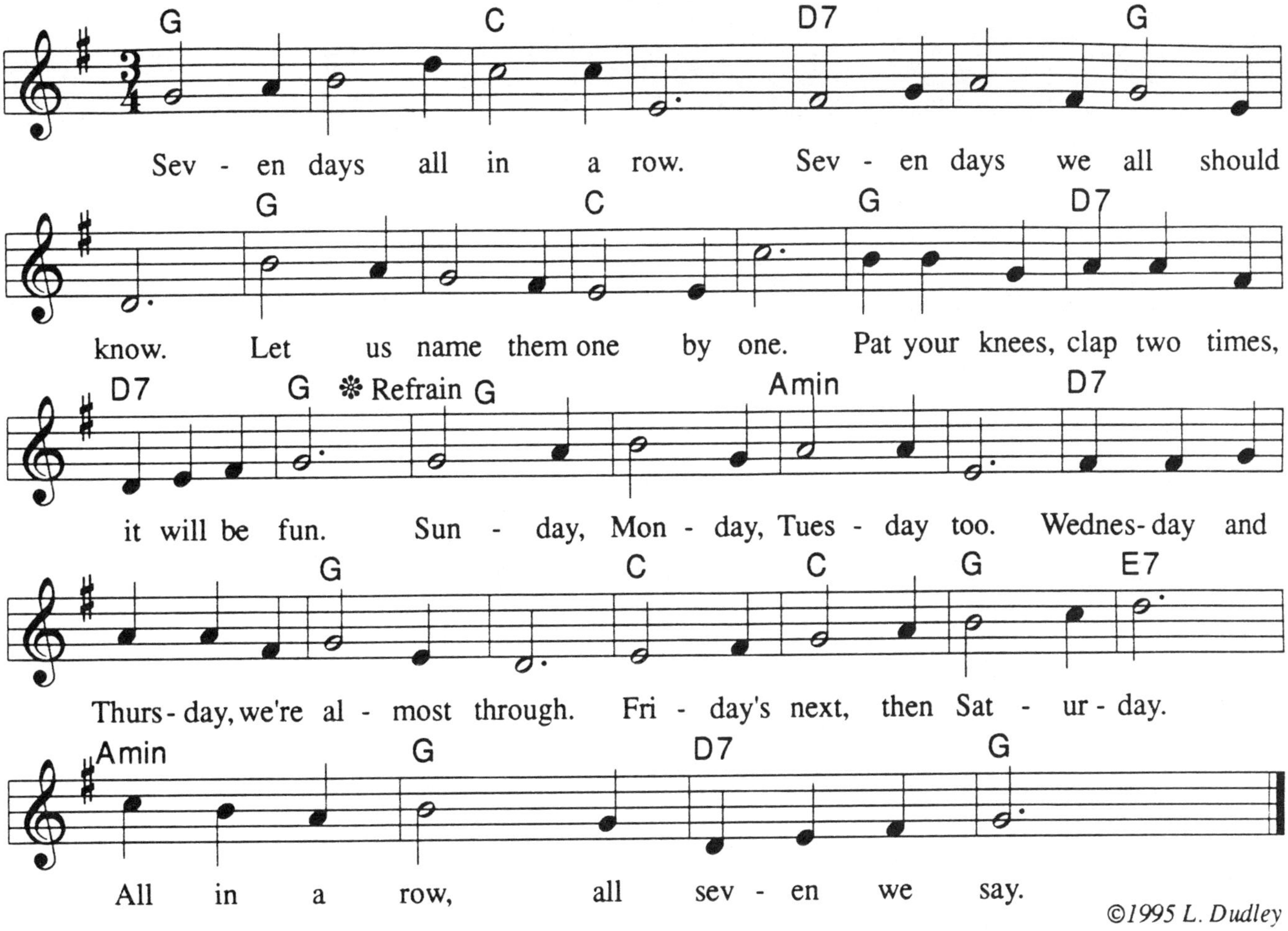

©1995 L. Dudley

Chant: Sunday, Monday, Tuesday, Wednesday, Thursday, Friday, Saturday

❊ Pat knees once, clap hands twice throughout refrain.

ACTIVITY

Mon. Tues. Wed. Thurs. Fri. Sat. Sun.

Write the abbreviations for each day of the week after the word of the week.

Monday ____________________ Friday ____________________

Tuesday ____________________ Saturday ____________________

Wednesday ____________________ Sunday ____________________

Thursday ____________________

 Read *The Very Hungry Caterpillar* by Eric Carle or another book about days of the week.

Who Am I?

Introduction
I may have had a long tail and feet with claws, I
Ped.
lived a mill-ion years a-go and sharp teeth filled my jaws. I
lived in the o-cean, on the land, or in the sky. My
name means "ter-ri-ble rep-tile," now who am I?

© 1995 L. Dudley

Who Am I?

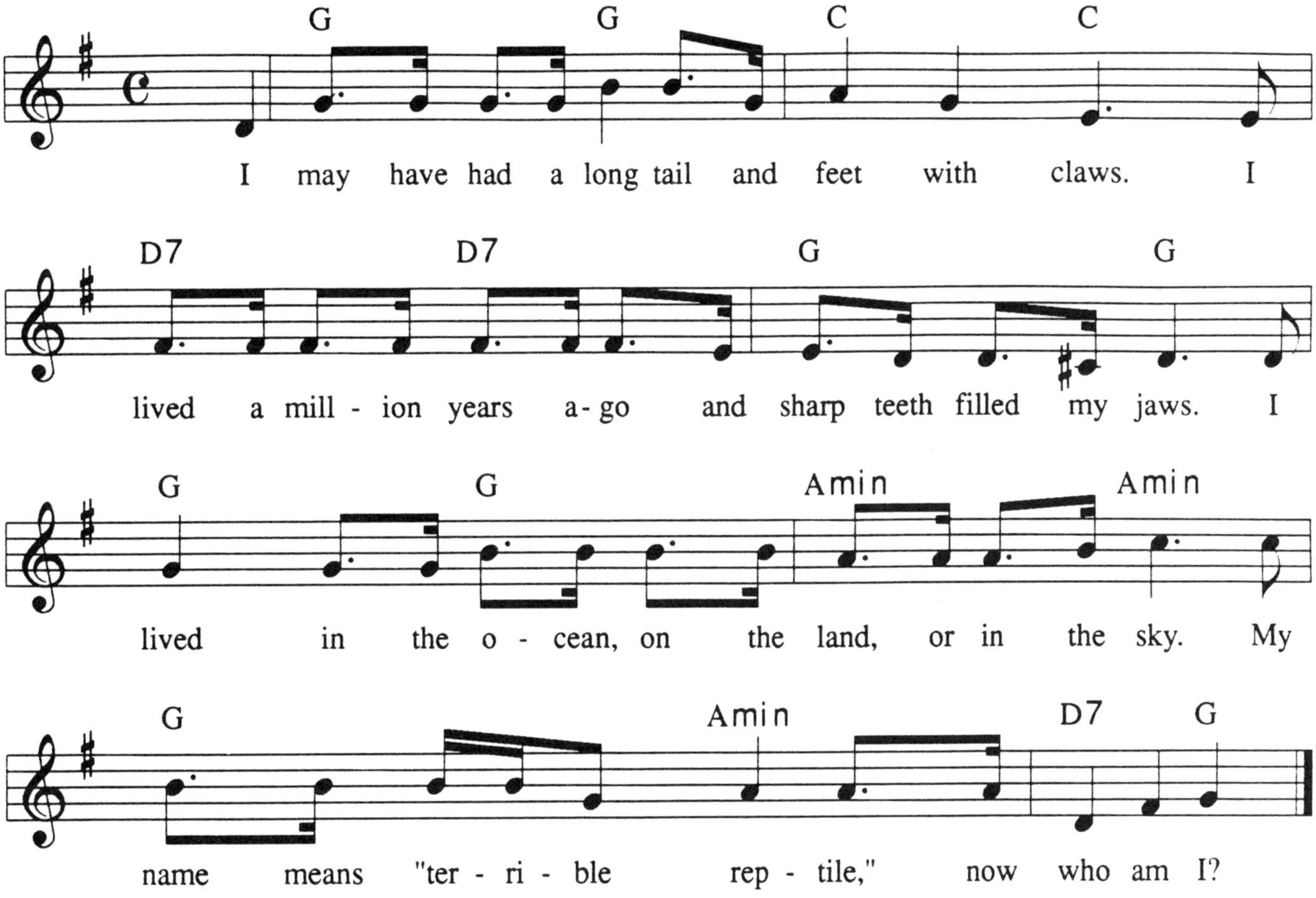
G G C C
I may have had a long tail and feet with claws. I
D7 D7 G G
lived a mill - ion years a- go and sharp teeth filled my jaws. I
G G Amin Amin
lived in the o - cean, on the land, or in the sky. My
G Amin D7 G
name means "ter - ri - ble rep - tile," now who am I?

© 1995 L. Dudley

ACTIVITY

Draw and color a picture to show the answer to the riddle.

Read *The Funniest Dinosaur Book Ever!* by Joseph Rosenbloom or another book about dinosaurs.

Woolly Bear

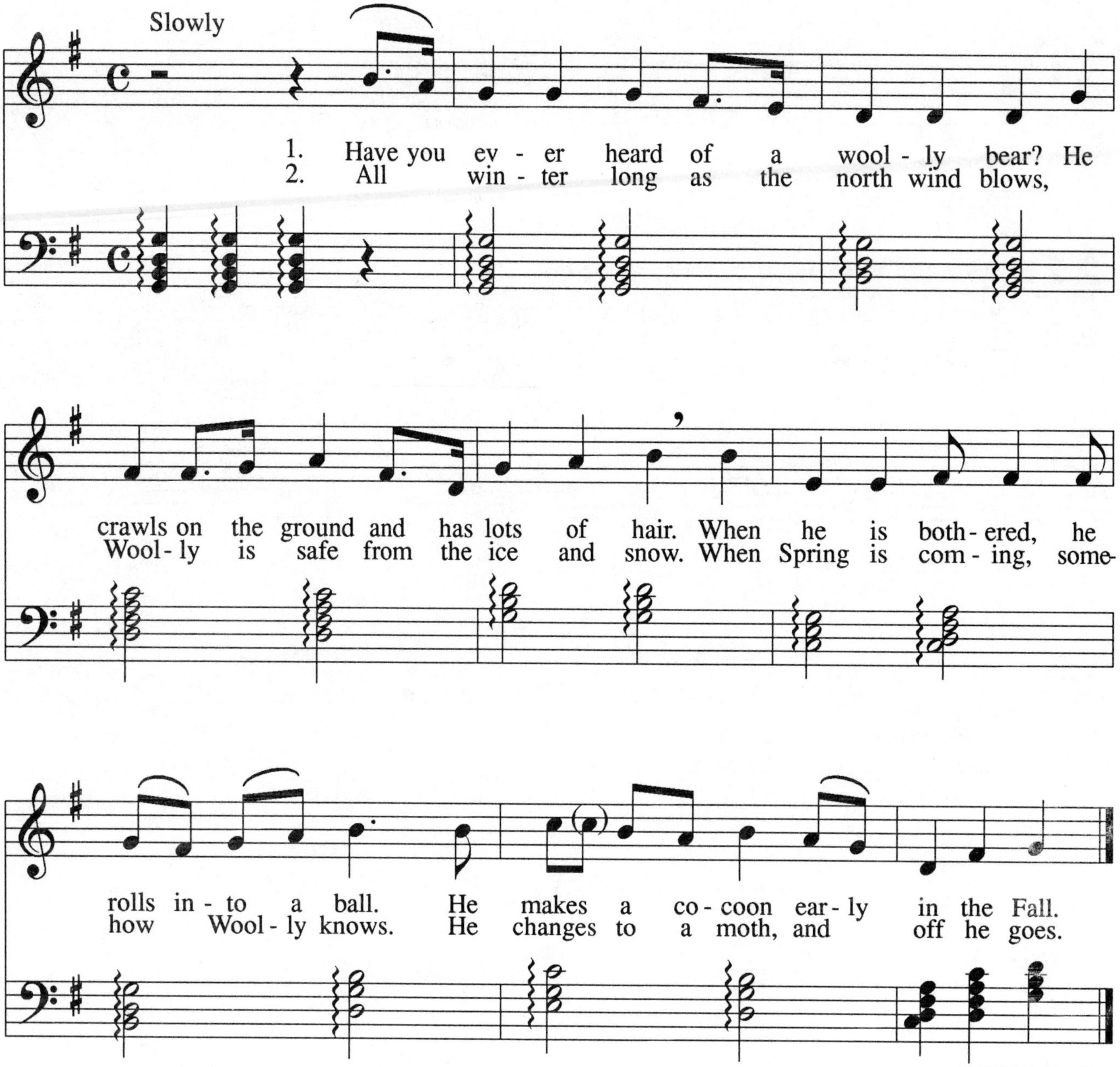
Slowly
1. Have you ev - er heard of a wool - ly bear? He
2. All win - ter long as the north wind blows,
crawls on the ground and has lots of hair. When he is both - ered, he
Wool - ly is safe from the ice and snow. When Spring is com - ing, some-
rolls in - to a ball. He makes a co - coon ear - ly in the Fall.
how Wool - ly knows. He changes to a moth, and off he goes.

©1995 L. Dudley

Woolly Bear

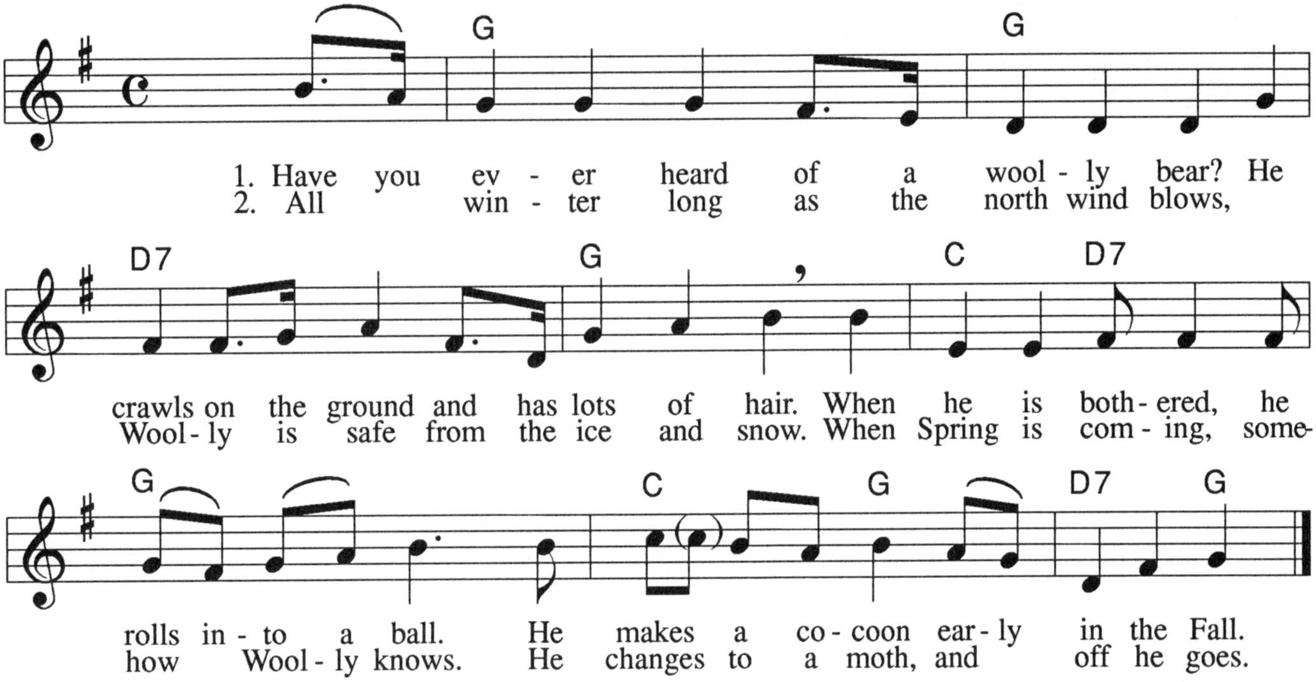
G G
1. Have you ev - er heard of a wool - ly bear? He
2. All win - ter long as the north wind blows,
D7 G C D7
crawls on the ground and has lots of hair. When he is both - ered, he
Wool - ly is safe from the ice and snow. When Spring is com - ing, some-
G C G D7 G
rolls in - to a ball. He makes a co - coon ear - ly in the Fall.
how Wool - ly knows. He changes to a moth, and off he goes.

©1995 L. Dudley

ACTIVITY

Look up the term 'woolly bear' in the dictionary. Write the definition in the space below.

____

____

____

____

____

Read *A First Look at Caterpillars* by Millicent E. Selsam or another book about caterpillars.

The Zoo

❊ Jungle noises
X=clap hands
There were rhi - nos, hy - e - nas, a
kan - ga - roo. Co - bras, and pan - das, a white tailed gnu.
Mon - keys, sea li - ons, and hip-pos too. Where did we go?
Where did we go? To the Zoo!

© 1995 L. Dudley

❊ Children can growl, imitate birds, roar, etc. as teacher counts to seven.

The Zoo

X=clap hands
C
Dmin
G7
There were rhin- os, hy - e- nas, a kang- a- roo. Cob- ras, and pan- das, a
C
C
F
white tailed gnu. Mon - keys, sea li - ons, and hip- pos too.
G7
G7
G7
C
Where did we go? Where did we go? To the Zoo!

© 1995 L. Dudley

SPELL AND TELL

Ask an adult to spell the name of an animal in the zoo. You say the name of the animal as you picture it in your mind.

THE
ZOO

Read *Zoo* by Gail Gibbons or another book about a zoo.

Books and Songs Index

Music and Topic Index

The following are suggestions for integrating songs with specific topics.

Possibilities for Using Instruments

Bubbles: Children may use a hand drum or rhythm sticks on the word *POP*.

A Builder: Children may wish to use instruments on the words *saw*, *tap*, *whirr*, and *zap*.

Butterflies: Children might use finger cymbals to end the song.

Friends Around the World: Children may play tambourines when singing the words *wiggle* and *giggle*.

It's Raining: Children may use a bell or triangle to give the effect of raindrops.

The Ocean: Children might use sand blocks on the steady beat.

A Rainbow: Children may use a wind chime or triangle to represent the rain.

Time: Children may use rhythm instruments for the tick-tock effect of the clock.

Toy Train: Children may use a whistle or a kazoo to represent the train whistle in the song.

Dear Parents

From time to time a song sheet from the book *Songs to Sing and Picture* will be sent home with your child. The children in our class have sung the song and have usually participated in an activity that relates to the song. Perhaps your child would like to sing the song for you. If you have a piano or a guitar, you might want to play the song as your child sings. A family sing-along is fun, too. You may want to save the song sheets so that you can make a booklet for your child to keep as his/her own music book.

Thank You.

Sincerely,

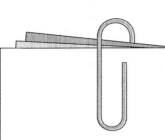

About the Authors

LILLIAN L. DUDLEY

Lillian (Bunny) Dudley earned a Bachelor of Science degree in music from Doane College (Crete, Nebraska) and a Master of Music from the University of Nebraska (Lincoln, Nebraska). She taught kindergarten for eight years, and is currently teaching elementary music (K-6) in the Crete public schools and music education at Doane College. She has published articles in the *Music Education Journal, Nebraska Choral Director's Journal*, and the *Alaskan Music Educator*. She also composed the anthem "All on a Christmas Day" for children's voices and/or instruments, published by Choristers Guild. Lillian has co-authored a book for elementary students, *After School Adventures*, and presented numerous workshops on various musical topics, such as music for exceptional children and preschool music and movement.

HARRIET R. KINGHORN

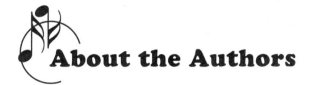

Harriet Kinghorn has taught in Nebraska and Minnesota elementary schools. She taught preschool, kindergarten, grades two through four, and enrichment classes. Harriet attended Doane College in Crete, Nebraska, for two years. She holds the degrees of Bachelor of Science in Education from the University of Nebraska and a Master of Science in Education from the University of North Dakota. Harriet has published in various educational magazines. She has also authored and co-authored numerous educational books, including *At Day's End: Book-Related Activities for Small Groups* (with Fay Hill Smith; Libraries Unlimited, 1988), *Every Child a Storyteller: A Handbook of Ideas* (with Mary Helen Pelton; Teacher Ideas Press, 1991), and *Handy Dandy Reading Records* (Teacher Ideas Press, 1996). Harriet was honored as "Teacher of the Year" in East Grand Forks, Minnesota, and as one of twelve "Honor Teachers" of Minnesota in 1976. Harriet received the Doane College Alumni Educator of the Year Award in 1994. Harriet is presently living in Westminster, Colorado, where she is writing and presenting workshops.